The Walter Lynwood Fleming
Lectures in Southern History
Louisiana State University

The South and Three Sectional Crises

The South
and Three
Sectional Crises

Don E. Fehrenbacher

Louisiana State University Press
Baton Rouge and London

Designer: Patricia Douglas Crowder
Typeface: VIP Electra
Typesetter: G & S Typesetters, Inc.
Printer: Thomson-Shore, Inc.
Binder: John Dekker & Sons, Inc.

LIBRARY OF CONGRESS CATALOGING IN PUBLICATION DATA

Fehrenbacher, Don Edward, 1920–
    The South and three sectional crises.
    (Walter Lynwood Fleming lectures in southern history)
    Includes bibliographical references and index.
    CONTENTS: The Missouri controversy and the sources of southern
sectionalism.—The Wilmot proviso and the mid-century crisis.—Kansas,
Republicanism, and the crisis of the Union.
    1. Missouri compromise—Addresses, essays, lectures. 2. Wilmot
proviso, 1846—Addresses, essays, lectures. 3. Kansas—History—1854–
1861—Addresses, essays, lectures. 4. Sectionalism (United States)—Addresses, essays, lectures. I. Title. II. Series.
E373.F43   973.7′113   79-18143
ISBN 0-8071-0671-2

To my sister and brothers:
Shirley, Bob, and Marvin

Contents

Preface

◈————

One writes a lecture listening to the sound of it, knowing that the words will be heard before they are read. Clarity and liveliness are at a premium; comprehensiveness is usually out of the question; and accuracy may suffer—especially the kind of accuracy that qualifies every generalization and rehearses the complexities of the subject. There is consequently much to be said for revising and expanding lectures before committing them to print, but in this instance I have chosen to forego the opportunity. The reason, quite simply, is diffidence in the face of the accumulated complexity of the literature on the causes of the Civil War. That is, I have been governed by the expectation that any such enterprise of expansion, once begun, might be extremely difficult to terminate. Except, then, for some changes of a formal nature (such as separating my introductory remarks from the body of the first lecture), the following pages reproduce my three Walter Lynwood Fleming Lectures in Southern History, just as I presented them at Louisiana State University on April 17 and 18, 1978. For the warm hospitality extended to me and my wife on that occasion, I thank the University and its Department of History, and particularly John L. and Helen Loos and Mark T. and Maureen Carleton. I am also grateful to Lewis P. Simpson for arranging publication of the first lecture in the *Southern Review*. In preparing the book for publication, I have had, as usual, much help from my wife Virginia, and I have enjoyed the gracious cooperation of the staff of the LSU Press.

The South and Three Sectional Crises

Introduction

My sectional credentials for the occasion were not impressive. Born in Illinois of parents likewise born in Illinois, I was educated in Illinois and Iowa and have lived for the past quarter of a century in California (not even Southern California at that). As a historian, I have written much more about Abraham Lincoln than about Jefferson Davis or Robert E. Lee. *And* my great-grandfather, Corporal George W. Outman of the 73rd Regiment of Illinois Volunteer Infantry, was killed by a Rebel sniper on New Year's Eve, 1862, leaving behind him a widow and three small children. Nevertheless, despite this inappropriate personal background, I recently had the honor of delivering the thirty-ninth Walter Lynwood Fleming Lectures in Southern History at Louisiana State University. It is no doubt safe to say that such a thing could happen only in America.

Let it be added, however, that I can claim one important southern connection. In graduate school at the University of Chicago, my teacher and dissertation director was a famous historian of the South, Avery O. Craven—the only scholar to serve twice as the Fleming Lecturer. His first series of lectures, presented in 1938 and entitled "The Repressible Conflict," became a landmark in the historiography of the Civil War. Returning in 1958, he addressed himself to the same subject with the title "Civil War in the Making"; for Craven was, of all American historians, the most persistent in his efforts to understand the disruption of the Union. Thus, in 1978, forty years after his first appearance as Fleming Lecturer and twenty years after his second, it seemed appropriate that one of Avery Craven's students should likewise venture a brief exploration of that treacherous scholar's jungle, the background of the Civil War.

Study of the subject is no longer as fashionable as it was when Craven, James G. Randall, Allan Nevins, Roy F. Nichols, David M. Potter, Kenneth M. Stampp, and others were all working the vein of historical ore that runs from the Wilmot Proviso to the firing on Fort Sumter; when the forays of Bernard DeVoto, Arthur M. Schlesinger, Jr., Frank L. Owsley, and Pieter Geyl were enlivening the tangled argument over causation; and when every scholar in the field was expected to take a stand on the question of whether the Civil War was or was not avoidable.

The battle of interpretations ran its course, becoming increasingly recapitulative and sterile. Civil War causation lost much of its intellectual appeal, and in 1960 David Herbert Donald pronounced it "dead" as a subject of scholarly investigation.[1] Four years later, at the age of seventy-eight, Avery Craven wryly acknowledged the "futility of trying to understand and explain the causes of the American Civil War."[2] At about the same time, Joel H. Silbey, speaking as a practitioner of the so-called "new political history," declared that scholarly emphasis on the coming of the Civil War had perniciously "distorted the reality" of antebellum politics by exaggerating the incidence and influence of sectional rivalry.[3]

In 1974, Eric Foner, after noting the impressive quantity and quality of recent scholarship on racism, slavery, and abolitionism, nevertheless concluded that explanation of the coming of the Civil War had made little progress since Donald's pronouncement in 1960. The problem, in his view, was poverty of conceptualization. "Discussion of the causes of the Civil War," he wrote, "continues to be locked into an antiquated interpretive framework. Historians of the Civil War era seem to be in greater need of new models of interpretation and new questions than of an additional accumulation of data." As an example of the kind of innovative thinking that is needed, Foner pointed to the concept of "modernization" and more specifically to the view of the Civil War as "the process by which the 'modern' or 'modernizing' North integrated the 'pre-modern' South into a national political and economic system."[4]

Such new models of interpretation for old historical problems are often synthetic and modish, however, reflecting the latest fashions in behavioral science theory and terminology but adding little to the substance of explanation. The concept of "modernization," in so far as it can be used to explain the coming of the Civil War, was largely anticipated by Avery Craven in sentences like this one written in 1964: "The real tragedy lies in the fact that these people [that is, the people of the antebellum South] remained socially and intellectually *comfortably* where they were, while the whole Western world, of which cotton made them a part, rushed headlong into the modern world of nationalism, industrial capitalism, democratic advancement, and a new respect for human rights."[5]

One virtue of the modernization model, according to Foner, is that it "enables us to see that what happened in nineteenth century America was not a unique or local occurrence, but a process which had deep affinities with events in many other areas of the world."[6] Yet the American experience was in some respects unique; for, as Carl N. Degler wrote in 1970: "The United States is the only country that required a civil war to ʳadicate slavery."[7] In short, the concept of "modernization," ᵗh its wide range of implications (including industrialization, ᵤᵣbanization, national integration, and psychological adaptation to rapid social change) may help us to understand why American slavery came to an end, but not why it came to a violent end.

What caused the Civil War is not a single historical problem but rather a whole cluster of problems, too numerous and complex to be incorporated into any single model of historical interpretation. For example, one crucial question, which has been answered most fully by David Brion Davis, is why Negro slavery, after several hundred years of respectable existence, suddenly came under fierce moral attack.[8] But no explanation of the origins of abolitionism will suffice to explain the emergence of a mass antislavery political organization in the 1850s. And, in turn, satisfactory reasons for the birth of the Republican party would not be enough to explain the Republican electoral triumph in 1860.

No more than the coming of the French Revolution is the coming of the American Civil War likely to be abandoned as a subject of historical inquiry in the lifetime of anyone now living; for there continues to be a great emotional investment in remembrance of the conflict, and every generation of Americans seems to discover some new understanding of itself in studying the spectacular and tragic disruption of the American Union. As for making progress toward better causal explanation, perhaps it is less important to invent new questions than to phrase some of the old questions more carefully and pursue the answers more diligently and rigorously.

Most discussion of the causes of the Civil War tends to concentrate on the causes of southern secession, in spite of the fact that armed conflict actually resulted from northern unwillingness to acquiesce in peaceable separation. Explanation of secession, though by no means the whole of the matter, is undoubtedly the heart of the matter. For secession was the most venturesome and extraordinary action in the sectional crisis— the one requiring the greatest amount of initiative—the bigges step into the unknown. But precisely what is meant by the term "southern secession"? The author of a recently published book falls into a common habit when he speaks of "the exuberance and confidence with which the South seceded."[9] The South, of course, did not secede. It was South Carolina that did so—South Carolina alone, followed in order by Mississippi, Florida, and Alabama; then by Georgia, Louisiana, and Texas; and later, after the guns had sounded in Charleston Harbor, by Virginia, Arkansas, Tennessee, and North Carolina. In addition, Kentucky and Missouri were claimed as parts of the Confederacy, but they are generally counted with Delaware and Maryland among the slaveholding states that did not secede at all.

The Civil War was precipitated, then, by the secession of just seven state governments, acting sequentially and representing less than one-third of the free population of the entire South. The number of secessions before Lincoln's inauguration probably fell within a critical range as far as the danger of war was concerned. That is, if only three or four states had seceded, such a feeble effort might well have ended peacefully in failure, whereas, if twelve or thirteen states had seceded before Lincoln's inauguration, such a formidable movement might well have ended peacefully in success. It is possible that seven was the optimum number of secessions for starting a civil war, and it may be that Virginia's initial failure to secede was as much a cause of war as South Carolina's headlong leadership in the secession movement.

Therefore, in explaining the causes of the Civil War, perhaps one ought to emphasize secessionism in seven of the southern states and antisecessionism in the other eight. Certainly there is good reason to differentiate southern states according to their behavior in the secession crisis and then keep the principal categories strictly in mind throughout any study of the sectional conflict. Those categories are: the seven states of the Lower

South that seceded after Lincoln's election; the four states of the Middle South that seceded after the firing on Fort Sumter; and the four states of the Border South that did not secede at all. In these three regions respectively, slaves were 46 percent, 29 percent, and 14 percent of the total population.[10] Of course the Lower South and Middle South together made up the Confederate South. The eight states of the Middle and Border Souths combined may be called the Upper South. And all three regions taken together constituted the fifteen states of the Slaveholding South.

There is another, more abstract problem of method that I would like to discuss before proceeding to a review of southern participation in the three great sectional crises of 1819–1821, 1846–1850, and 1854–1861. Avery Craven sometimes insisted that his purpose was not to explain the causes of the Civil War but rather merely to explain "how events got into such shape that they could not be handled by the democratic process."[11] Critics did not take the protestation very seriously, and Craven himself repeatedly blurred the distinction he sought to draw. A differentiation between *causes* and the *shape of events* may be unsound and ultimately unmanageable, but it has a special usefulness as a way of looking at the background of the Civil War.

Craven was talking about the problem of how historical causes are so activated as to produce their consequences—how attitudes and purposes are crystallized into action. The Civil War had no real equivalent of the skirmishes at Lexington and Concord. It did not flare up out of local violence and spread across the land. Apparently there was never much danger that it *would* begin in such a way—not even as a result of John Brown's inflammatory adventure at Harpers Ferry. The accumulation of sectional hostility in antebellum America was translated into civil war through the intermedium of secession. And secession, though fraught with passion, was nevertheless not only nonviolent but highly formal. So formal, in fact, as to increase substantially the difficulty of setting it in motion. Secession could not be provoked by any informal outburst of sectional animosity, such as that associated with the Harpers Ferry raid, but only by a formal public act or action of major import, such as passage of a federal law. The famous Georgia platform of 1850 listed six eventualities, any one of which would be sufficient cause for disunion, and all six were apprehended actions of Congress. [12]

We might therefore visualize the accumulating sectional hostility as a charge of explosive that grew to be enormous in its destructive potential but was never extremely unstable. It could not be set off by a random spark like a dust-filled grain elevator. Instead, the explosion required the formality of a detonator or fuse. I believe that Craven's distinction between causes and the shape of events was essentially a distinction between charge and fuse. I also believe that the highly formal nature of secession makes the distinction especially helpful in study of the coming of the Civil War; for in a sense the decisive change that took place in the late 1850s was not the ominous continuing increase in the size of the charge, but rather the introduction of a new and more effective fuse.

1 The Missouri Controversy and the Sources of Southern Sectionalism

Historians generally agree that the Missouri controversy of 1819–1821 was a turning point in the history of the sectional conflict, but they differ about what phase it constituted in the development of southern distinctiveness and self-awareness. James A. Woodburn called the struggle "the first clear demarcation between the sections."[1] Clement Eaton said that in political terms, the South "did not begin until 1820."[2] Charles S. Sydnor suggested that it might be anachronistic to use the word "southerners" for the time before 1819; for, as he put it, "regional differences had not borne the evil fruit of sectional bitterness."[3] On the other hand, Jesse T. Carpenter dated his study of *The South as a Conscious Minority* from the year 1789 and insisted, indeed, that "the inhabitants of those states below the Mason and Dixon line always considered themselves a separate and distinct people."[4] Also, John R. Alden in his Fleming Lectures undertook to demonstrate the historical reality of what he called the First South. "It appeared," he said, "with the American nation; it was christened as early as 1778; and it clashed ever more sharply with a First North during and immediately after the War of Independence."[5]

The disagreement between these scholars is partly one of their criteria and emphases, but it also reflects a cyclical pattern in the awakening of the South. That is, to some historians the Missouri Compromise looks like the beginning of southern sectionalism because in certain respects it was a *new* beginning of that phenomenon.

The underlying social and economic differences between the northern and southern colonies inspired open political rivalry from the formation of the Republic; and political rivalry, in turn, was the principal stimulant of sectional consciousness. In 1776, during early stages of work on the Articles of Confederation, members of the Continental Congress engaged in a sharp debate on the question of whether slaves should be counted in the apportionment of taxes. The division was almost totally along sectional lines. The same issue, tied to the problem of representation in Congress, troubled the deliberations of the Constitutional Convention in 1787, until the matter was at last settled by adoption of the three-fifths compromise. Yet slavery, though defended vehemently at times, especially by representatives of South Carolina and Georgia, was not the primary subject of contention between North and South during the first quarter century of independence.

More serious were the sectional quarrels over navigation of the Mississippi River, over Alexander Hamilton's financial program for the new nation, and over Jay's treaty with Great Britain, negotiated in 1794. Mounting southern opposition to the Federalist regime stemmed primarily from the conviction that national policies were favoring northern commercial enterprise at the expense of southern agriculture. "We are completely under the saddle of Massachusetts and Connecticut," said Thomas Jefferson in 1798. "They ride us very hard, cruelly insulting our feelings as well as exhausting our strength and subsistence."[6] The emergence of the Jeffersonian Republican opposition as an organized political party was to no small degree a sectional event. In the presidential election of 1796, Jefferson won fifty out of fifty-two electoral votes in the states south of Maryland; John Adams won all fifty-one electoral votes in the states north of Pennsylvania; and the thirty-six votes of New Jersey, Pennsylvania, Delaware, and Maryland were divided equally between them.

One way that the sectionalism of the 1790s foreshadowed the sectionalism of the 1850s was in the widespread fear of conspiracy on both sides. The Alien and Sedition acts confirmed many Republicans in their suspicion of a Federalist design to crush freedom of dissent and establish a monarchy. Jefferson predicted that the next step would be an attempt to make Adams president for life.[7] On the other hand, the famous resolutions of Virginia and Kentucky attacking the Alien and Sedition acts only strengthened the conviction of many Federalists that Republican leaders were engaged in a treasonable plot to overthrow the Constitution and turn the United States into an appendage of Revolutionary France.

Within this context of intense partisan conflict, southerners in the 1790s did indeed have a growing sense of being mistreated as a section (though not on account of slavery), and their protests sometimes had the ring of prophecy. The Virginia and Kentucky Resolutions laid out the doctrines of strict construction, state sovereignty, and nullification. And among some Virginians there was apparently talk of secession and even of armed resistance to federal power. But the resolutions were not intended as blueprints for any organized southern action, except action at the polls. They were, in practical terms, campaign literature. Jefferson's goal was not a united South but control of the federal government. When that was achieved in 1800, much of the reason for southern sectionalism disappeared, and New England became the nation's conscious minority, ridden hard under a Virginia saddle.

With southern political power ascendant, the Jeffersonian

era was a period without parallel in the territorial expansion of slavery. Jefferson himself did little to prevent it, and, in fact, he came to embrace the popular southern argument that a wide diffusion of slavery would benefit the slave population and the nation as a whole. In 1784, he had proposed that the institution be prohibited in the entire trans-Appalachian West, but as president he made no effort to secure the exclusion of slavery from the Louisiana Purchase. On the contrary, the plan for the government of Louisiana that he sent to Congress in November 1803 included a rigorous slave code.[8]

Like a good many other enlightened Virginians of the Revolutionary generation, Jefferson had long since gone inactive in his opposition to slavery. Racial preconceptions and fears, as well as political considerations, had blunted his lifelong hatred of the institution and driven him to the conviction that the problem could be solved only by the slow working of time.[9] He headed a political party of predominantly southern interest, but one that needed northern allies to control the presidency and Congress. The Jeffersonian Republicans, like their successors the Jacksonian Democrats, accordingly had good reason to muffle the issue of slavery, and northern members of the party were under strong though usually tacit pressure to restrain whatever antislavery feelings they may have had.

The Jeffersonian silence on domestic slavery was not sectionally neutral in its effect on westward expansion; for previous legislation dating back to 1790 had established the rule that slaveholding could be practiced anywhere in federal territory if it was not positively forbidden by federal law. This was doubly true of Louisiana, where slavery had been legal under both French and Spanish dominion. The Jeffersonians were consequently able to legitimate slaveholding throughout the whole of Louisiana simply by passing territorial organic acts that contained no provisions excluding it.

The strongest antislavery resistance arose in 1804. A proposal to limit (but not to abolish) slavery in Orleans Territory was defeated in the Senate by a vote of seventeen to eleven, with northern Federalists and northern Republicans both fairly evenly divided, while southerners provided the margin of defeat. During the next fifteen years, slavery continued to expand across the Mississippi as far north as St. Louis, without provoking sectional controversy.[10]

Furthermore, slavery in several other respects seemed securely linked to the nation's destiny. The vitality of the institution was indicated by its continued existence in Illinois and Indiana more than thirty years after it had been officially prohibited there. Southerners could take their household slaves with them into free states for extended visits—up to nine months by law in New York, for example. The national capital was a slaveholding community, with a slave code enforced by federal authority, and the United States, in its relations with foreign powers, conducted itself as a slaveholding nation. The very power and respectability of the slavery interest, which had not been seriously challenged for more than a decade, made the shock of the Missouri crisis all the greater for southerners when it came.

Just why northern members of Congress, after so many years of passivity, chose to take a stand in 1819 is still an open question among historians. As late as April 1818, a proposal to forbid slavery in all states thereafter admitted was quickly smothered in the House of Representatives.[11] Yet, within ten months, antislavery sentiment had swept into control of the chamber and precipitated the first sectional crisis over slavery. It did make a difference, of course, to have the War of 1812 ended and Europe generally at peace after a quarter century of upheaval and conflict. With American interest turning inward after 1815, a renewal of national self-scrutiny was bound to include consideration of the paradox of slavery in a nation formally dedicated to the principle that all men are created equal. Many northern congressmen seem to have awakened more or less suddenly to a realization that slavery had come to be fearfully predominant in the design of the nation's future. For confirmation they needed only to look at the boundaries proposed for the new state of Missouri, which would carry the institution northward two hundred miles above the mouth of the Ohio River.

To be sure, political motives also played their part. Jefferson's overwrought suspicion, shared by Madison and Monroe, that the Missouri controversy sprang from Federalist ambition to regain power, was not entirely groundless. Yet a Federalist effort alone could not have produced a crisis. It was the antislavery solidarity of so many northern Republicans that dismayed the South and inspired a new surge in the development of southern consciousness. The weakness of Federalism as a national party had slackened the need for loyalty and discipline within the Republican organization, thus making members of Congress more amenable to sectional pressures. It was not just accident that the Missouri crisis coincided with the demise of the first American party system.[12]

In spite of Jefferson's famous comparison of the crisis to "a fire bell in the night," there were some intimations in 1818 of what was soon to come. An attempt to pass a more stringent fugitive-slave law ended in failure, but not before it had provoked a good deal of sectional feeling. Later in the year, Congressman James Tallmadge, Jr., spoke out against a bill admitting Illinois to statehood. He argued that slavery was not "sufficiently pro-hibited" in the Illinois constitution, and about one-third of the northern congressmen joined him in voting against admission.[13]

It was this same James Tallmadge, a New York Republican of the disaffected Clintonian faction, who set off the Missouri struggle in February 1819. To a proposed enabling act for Missouri, he offered an amendment prohibiting the further introduction of slavery and providing that slave children born after the date of admission should be free at the age of twenty-five. Note that Tallmadge was not proposing emancipation of the ten thousand slaves already held in Missouri. His amendment amounted to a program of gradual abolition that would have extended over more than half a century.

With southern members almost unanimous in their opposition, the House of Representatives approved both parts of the Tallmadge proviso.[14] What followed is a familiar chapter in American history. The Senate struck the proviso from the bill. The House refused to concur. The Senate insisted, and again the House refused to concur. Congress adjourned in March with the issue unsettled and the angry debate resounding across the country. A new Congress convened in December 1819, but the two houses quickly discovered that they were no nearer agreement on the Missouri question. After more than two months of further debate, a compromise package was put together and approved in the Senate, then accepted piecemeal by the House. It comprised the admission of Maine as a free state and an enabling act for Missouri without restriction on slavery, together with the provision that in the remaining federal territory acquired from France, slavery should be "forever prohibited" north of latitude 36° 30'.[15]

The crisis accordingly appeared to be at an end, but it was furiously renewed a year later when Missouri applied for admission with a constitution that forbade free Negroes to enter the state. Again, heated debate extended over several months. Maine having already been admitted to statehood, southerners accused northerners of bad faith in setting up an additional barrier to the admission of Missouri. At last both houses of Congress accepted the terms of a second Missouri Compromise, which ambiguously guaranteed citizens the right to enter Missouri without saying whether free blacks were citizens.[16]

In many obvious ways, the two-year struggle anticipated

the sectional argument and the sectional anger of the late ante-bellum period, but it is important to note differences as well as similarities. The first Missouri controversy, in 1819–1820, was primarily over the power of Congress to set conditions on the admission of a state. The second, in 1821, was over the rights of free Negroes. As for the issue that would later preoccupy so much public discussion—namely, the power of Congress over slavery in the territories—it never assumed critical importance and rose when it did chiefly in connection with Arkansas, rather than in the Missouri debates. Legislation for the organization of Arkansas Territory, made necessary by the prospective admission of Missouri, proceeded through Congress virtually in tandem with the ill-fated Missouri bill of 1819. Discussion of the two measures became somewhat intermixed because antislavery leaders tried several times without success to fasten the Tallmadge restrictions on Arkansas.

Now, the Missouri debate tended to be heavily constitutional, involving several fundamental questions about the relationship between federal power and state sovereignty. And to some extent this tendency spilled over into the debate on Arkansas. Previously, the constitutional authority of Congress over slavery in the territories (which rested, after all, on a body of legislative precedent dating back to the Northwest Ordinance) had never been significantly challenged. During the Arkansas debate and even at some points in the Missouri controversy, a number of southerners did question that authority, and a few, like the future president John Tyler, emphatically denied it.[17] These were but random beginnings, however, of the great constitutional debate that would convulse the nation by mid-century. In 1819, southern congressmen relied more on other arguments, such as economic necessity and sectional equity, to justify slaveholding in Arkansas. Probably a majority of them still had little doubt of congressional power to exclude slavery from the territories, and, indeed, many of them implicitly acknowledged the power by voting for the 36° 30′ restriction.

The efforts in the House of Representatives to impose antislavery restrictions on Arkansas Territory failed by very narrow margins. The House passed the territorial organization bill and sent it on to the Senate just three days after having passed and sent on the Missouri enabling bill with the Tallmadge amendment attached. By making no attempt to unite the two measures, antislavery leaders in the House neglected an opportunity to use slavery in Arkansas as leverage against slavery in Missouri. The Senate simply passed the Arkansas bill (which was then signed into law by President James Monroe) while refusing to accept the Missouri bill unless the Tallmadge amendment were deleted. When a similar opportunity presented itself to the Senate a year later, there was no hesitation about using the admission of Maine as leverage against slavery restrictions on Missouri. More often than not in later times of sectional crisis, the power advantage of an antislavery majority in the House of Representatives would be neutralized by the superior parliamentary skills of its adversaries.

For that matter, the Missouri Compromise of 1820 was, in behavioral terms, no compromise at all but essentially a caving-in of the House's slender antislavery majority that had managed to block passage of the Missouri bill for more than a year. Southerners, in contrast, never failed to present a solid front where Missouri was concerned. On the crucial proposal to strike out the slavery restriction (which finally passed the House with just one vote to spare), combined voting of both houses, broken down by sections, was: northern members, 19 in favor and 102 against; southern members, 98 in favor and *none* against.[18]

In a sense, then, the only real compromisers were those nineteen northern members of Congress—and more particularly, the fourteen in the House—who forced their section to yield on the critical issue. But assignment of responsibility for the Missouri Compromise is not so easily accomplished. To begin with, there is a problem of terminology. The admission of Maine in 1820 and Missouri in 1821, being irrevocable acts of Congress, quickly faded from public controversy and became matters of settled history instead. In later years, accordingly, the phrase "Missouri Compromise" was often used to designate only that part of the settlement of 1820 that remained operative —namely, the 36° 30' restriction by itself. Historians have generally followed the same practice. For instance, the Kansas-Nebraska Act of 1854 is commonly spoken of as having repealed the Missouri Compromise, whereas it actually repealed only the 36° 30' restriction. This confusion of terms has led some scholars to the mistaken belief that congressmen from the free states were the principal authors of compromise, for the sectional voting on the 36° 30' restriction in both houses combined was: northern members, 115 in favor and 7 opposed; southern members, 53 in favor and 45 opposed.[19] But the 36° 30' restriction was actually just one-half of one side of the compromise. A grossly uneven division of the remaining federal territory, it had been proposed originally during the Arkansas debates by John W. Taylor, an antislavery Republican from New York. Later, however, it was brought forward by proslavery strategists as a concession to the North—as part of the price to be paid for the admission of Missouri as a slaveholding state.

Of course the real compromise, if there really *was* a compromise, consisted of the Missouri bill, the Maine bill, and the 36° 30' restriction. Sectional attitudes are especially clear in the proceedings of the Senate, where the three measures were at one point voted on as a single package. Southerners supported the package, 20 to 2; northerners opposed it, 18 to 4. "The vote," says Glover Moore, "leaves no doubt about which section of the country favored and which did not favor the compromise of 1820."[20] But the vote does *not* mean that southern members of Congress were generally more reasonable and flexible than their northern colleagues. It means only that in this *particular* compromise plan, formulated by proslavery leaders, the South got what it wanted most and the North did not. The contest from the beginning was for the future of Missouri, with the 36° 30′ restriction added as a consolation prize.

In retrospect, southern willingness to surrender the vast area north of 36° 30′ is somewhat surprising. No doubt it reflected a low estimate of the region's potential value, especially for plantation agriculture. But in addition, most southerners and northerners alike seem to have been convinced that the Missouri bird in the hand was worth more than several birds in the territorial bush.

In the House of Representatives, where no vote was ever taken on the Compromise as a whole, the vote on the 36° 30′ restriction provides the best measure, though an imprecise one, of various attitudes within the southern delegation.[21] Southern representatives supported the restriction by the narrow margin of 39 to 37. The three border states (Delaware, Maryland, and Kentucky) voted 16 to 2 in favor; Virginia, 18 to 4 against; and the rest of the South, 19 to 17 in favor, with South Carolina contributing five affirmative votes and four negative ones.

Thus the center of proslavery extremism in 1820 was not the Lower South but Virginia, aptly described by Glover Moore as "a nation within a nation, eager to maintain its prestige and prerogatives."[22] Thomas Ritchie's Richmond *Enquirer* led the newspaper attack on the Compromise, insisting that the South must not allow itself to be browbeaten by the antislavery forces into ransoming Missouri by consenting to the 36° 30′ restriction. "Shall we," the *Enquirer* asked, "surrender so much of this region, that was nobly won by the councils of a Jefferson, and paid for out of a common treasury?" Warning that the precedent set would invite further sectional aggression, it added: "If we yield now, beware.—they will ride us forever." The *En-*

quirer greeted passage of the Compromise in March 1820 with the words, "We scarcely ever recollect to have tasted of a bitterer cup. . . . The door is henceforth slammed in our faces. . . . What is a *territorial* restriction to-day becomes a *state* restriction to-morrow." [23]

The 36° 30' restriction, though opposed by many southerners, provoked very little debate in either house. The restriction was not needed to get the Missouri bill through the Senate, and there is no clear evidence that it changed a single northern vote in the House of Representatives. As a generous concession to antislavery sentiment, it made things much easier for history's original "doughfaces"—the northerners who voted with the South—but they were motivated by other considerations. Senators Ninian Edwards and Jesse B. Thomas of Illinois, for example, voted with the South because they were themselves southerners and slaveholders. Henry Baldwin of Pennsylvania voted with the South in the hope of softening southern opposition to a higher tariff. Apparently several doughfaces agreed with the southern argument that imposing slavery restrictions on an incoming state would be unconstitutional. And apparently some northern Republicans were governed, like Jefferson, by deep suspicion of Federalist motives.

But what "perhaps did more than anything else to undermine Northern solidarity," says Glover Moore, was the fear of disunion. [24] Charles Kinsey of New Jersey, one of the handful of antislavery congressmen who determined the outcome of the struggle by switching to the southern side, gave eloquent expression to that fear in a speech delivered just before the decisive vote in the House. "On the next step we take depends the fate of unborn millions," he warned. Disunion, he said, presented itself "in all the horrid, gloomy features of reality," and a northern victory in the confrontation would be "an inglorious triumph, gained at the hazard of the Union." [25]

Throughout the crisis there was certainly a good deal of

southern talk about disunion and civil war, much of it in the form of flowery prediction rather than plain threat. Thus Senator Freeman Walker of Georgia envisioned "a brother's sword crimsoned with a brother's blood." And Thomas W. Cobb, another Georgian, declared that antislavery leaders had "kindled a fire which all the waters of the ocean" could not put out, and which only "seas of blood" could extinguish. [26] Yet the Missouri crisis was not a secession crisis, though it might have become one in time. Even the Richmond *Enquirer*, in bitterly accepting passage of the Compromise, acknowledged that the Union had never been in serious danger. [27] "If there had been a civil war in 1819–1821," says Moore, "it would have been between the members of Congress, with the rest of the country looking on in amazement." Moore goes on to suggest that "the Union would almost certainly have broken up at some time in the 1820's if . . . there had been an absolute refusal to compromise." [28] Perhaps so, but such a refusal, as he himself concludes, was a "remote possibility." For the longer the crisis lasted, the harder it became to keep Missouri out of the Union; and a truly imminent danger of disunion would have put unbearable pressure for compromise on many northern Republicans. Southerners did nevertheless begin to learn in the Missouri crisis how effectively the threat of disunion could be used as a weapon of southern defense.

The Missouri crisis in fact had many meanings and lessons for the South—some readily understood and others only vaguely sensed but often becoming clearer in the light of later events. For instance, the sudden appearance of an antislavery majority in the House of Representatives dramatically confirmed the southern need to maintain sectional equality in the Senate, but only dimly at best did any southerners in 1820 perceive the advantages of reestablishing a bisectional two-party system in national politics. The complaint of some southern congressmen that public discussion of the "delicate" subject of slavery increased the danger of slave revolts took on new meaning in 1822 after exposure of the Denmark Vesey conspiracy. It was not until the middle decades of the century, however, that the Missouri struggle came to be regarded as the beginning of southern degradation at the hands of the North. Thus Eli S. Shorter of Alabama would look back in anger from the floor of the House of Representatives in 1858: "We remember the compromise of 1820. The brand of inferiority was then stamped deep on the brow of southern manhood and southern honor; and there it remained, a burning disgrace, till the Kansas-Nebraska bill wiped it out and restored us to our long lost rights."[29]

In its constitutional aspects, the congressional debate on Missouri lent reinforcement to the old Republican preference for strict construction. The Tallmadge amendment, by proposing the gradual abolition of slavery in a prospective state *after* its admission to statehood, offered a much greater constitutional threat to the security of slavery than the Wilmot Proviso of later years. For, if antislavery spokesmen were right in asserting that any one of several clauses in the Constitution (such as the clause guaranteeing each state a republican form of government) could be construed as authorizing congressional regulation of slavery in a *new* state, what constitutional barrier remained to prevent the same kind of interference in the *oldest* of the slaveholding states? The Missouri struggle therefore connected antislavery sentiment more closely to broad construction and nationalism than it had ever been connected before. After 1820, it became increasingly difficult for a defender of slavery to support the expansion of federal power. John C. Calhoun managed to do so for just a few more years.

The Missouri debates also drew many a southerner unwillingly into discussion of the moral aspects of the slavery problem. Only a few militants like Senator William Smith of South Carolina defended the institution openly and absolutely, thus ushering in the "positive good" phase of proslavery ideology. For the most part, southern members of Congress were still willing to say that slavery was an evil—a curse, a cancer. Moore accordingly views the Missouri controversy as marking the end of an age in which southern thought had been dominated by the liberalism of the Enlightenment.[30]

Yet, upon close scrutiny, southern acknowledgment of the wrongness of slavery was largely an empty gesture in 1820. It had no effect on the main line of southern argument, which held the institution to be indispensable and ineradicable. The conflict between southern rhetoric and southern conviction was strikingly revealed in a speech by Congressman Robert Reid of Georgia. Reid at one point declared that the day when black Americans were given equal rights as citizens would be "most glorious in its dawning." But then he immediately added that such a "dream of philanthropy" could never be fulfilled, and that any person who acted upon such "wild theories" would become a "destroyer of the human family."[31]

The votes of southern congressmen in the Missouri struggle spoke more clearly than many of their speeches. Those votes indicated that the South had already made the most important decision in the whole history of the slavery controversy—and made it with virtual unanimity. That is, the Slaveholding South by 1820 had rejected the possibility of gradual emancipation, even in a new part of the country where it would have been neither impractical nor dangerous. It was this southern commitment to the *permanence* of slavery, and not the mere presence of slavery in the land, that made sectional conflict irrepressible and disunion increasingly probable as the nineteenth century advanced.

2 The Wilmot Proviso and the Mid-Century Crisis

Robert Toombs of Georgia was no typical fire-eater, but he spoke at times in flaming words. On December 13, 1849, Toombs warned the House of Representatives: "If by your legislation you seek to drive us from the territories of California and New Mexico . . . thereby attempting to fix a national degradation upon half the States of this Confederacy, *I am for disunion.*" Six months later he returned to the same theme, declaring:

I stand upon the great principle that the South has right to an equal participation in the territories of the United States. . . . She will divide with you if you wish it, but the right to enter all or divide I shall never surrender. . . . Deprive us of this right and appropriate this common property to yourselves, it is then your government, not mine. Then I am its enemy, and I will then, if I can, bring my children and my constituents to the altar of liberty, and like Hamilcar I would swear them to eternal hostility to your foul domination. Give us our just rights, and we are ready, as ever heretofore, to stand by the Union . . . Refuse it, and for one, I will strike for *Independence.*[1]

The crisis of 1846–1850 was truly a secession crisis—the first in American history. It began with the introduction of the

Wilmot Proviso and was the only sectional crisis ever precipitated by an effort to prohibit slavery in federal territory. From
the southern point of view, as Toombs so eloquently asserted
in Congress, it was a struggle to secure *equality* and to avoid
degradation. Those two words and their equivalents appear
repeatedly in southern speeches and editorials of the period.
Thus Albert Gallatin Brown of Mississippi declared that he pre-
ferred disunion to "social and sectional degradation." Abraham
W. Venable of North Carolina opposed the Compromise of
1850 because he considered it "degrading to the South." John
B. Lamar of Georgia spoke of being "degraded into inequality."
And Jefferson Davis after the Civil War said that the principal
cause of the conflict had been "the systematic and persistent
struggle to deprive the Southern States of equality in the
Union."[2]

Southern members of Congress had appealed frequently to
the principle of equality during the Missouri controversy, but
they were then talking primarily about constitutional equality
among the sovereign states of the Union, especially as it related to proposals for discriminatory restrictions on slaveholding
in the state of Missouri. Southerners at that time were obviously
less concerned about sectional equality in the territories; otherwise, a majority of them would not have supported the 36°
30′ restriction.

What southern leaders were demanding by mid-century was
equality between the North and the South viewed almost as
sovereign entities—equality most particularly in legal access
to the federal territories, but equality also in moral standing.
The bitter yearning for a lost respectability was well expressed by
John C. Calhoun when he declared: "I am a southern man and
a slaveholder; a kind and a merciful one, I trust—and none the
worse for being a slaveholder. . . . I would rather meet any ex-
tremity upon earth than give up one inch of our equality . . .

What, acknowledge inferiority! The surrender of life is nothing to sinking down into acknowledged inferiority."[3]

Historians for more than a century have pondered the sectional struggle over slavery in the territories, trying to explain how it came to be invested with an emotional intensity that seems far out of proportion to its practical significance. The sum of all their scholarship still does not tell us clearly why the antebellum generation pursued to its disastrous conclusion an argument that became increasingly abstruse and that in any case had largely been settled by the forces of nature.

Some writers have concluded that much of the northern opposition to the extension of slavery was animated by ulterior political and economic motives. Some have interpreted southern expansionism as a natural function of the dynamics of plantation agriculture, while others have emphasized southern determination to maintain a sectional balance in the Senate as a shield against congressional assaults on slavery. The territorial controversy has also been interpreted as a hastening descent into irrationality and as a symbolic conflict in which the real issue was the future of slavery itself. Certainly, it can be added that southerners came to regard the status of slavery in the territories as a measure of their success or failure in the struggle for equality. .

"The right to enter all or divide I shall never surrender," Toombs declared in 1850. Those were the only two bases for sectional equality in the territories. Either federal territory must *all* be open equally to northerners and to southerners (with their slaves), or it must be divided into northern and southern spheres of influence. The first alternative, though equitable in theory, was proslavery in its practical effects. For territory settled by a mixture of slaveholders and nonslaveholders became, as a matter of legal necessity, a slaveholding territory; and until 1861, all slaveholding territories became slaveholding states.

In providing governments for the trans-Appalachian West, Congress followed the policy of division. It prohibited slavery north of the Ohio River by reenacting the antislavery clause of the Northwest Ordinance. And it expressly exempted territories south of the river from the same clause, thus authorizing slavery by implication without officially establishing it. In providing governments for the Louisiana Purchase, however, Congress adopted the other policy, ostensibly neutral but actually pro-slavery, of opening the entire region to slaveholders and non-slaveholders alike. Furthermore, in the organization of Louisi-ana Territory (which became Missouri Territory in 1812 and covered all of the Purchase except the state of Louisiana), the policy was achieved by omitting *all* reference to slavery, even the familiar exemption from restriction that had become the rule in the Old Southwest. This was the Jeffersonian silence, embracing in purest form the principle that would later be called "nonintervention." It prevailed in the Louisiana Pur-chase until 1820. Then an upsurge of antislavery sentiment forced a return to the dual system, with slavery forbidden north of 36° 30′ and nonintervention silently continued south of that line.

Nonintervention, because of its negative character, was real-ly just the first half of a territorial policy. In practice, it led to popular sovereignty. That is, it left the question of slavery to be decided by the people settling a territory. They did so informally at first, simply by bringing or not bringing slaves with them, and then officially through the action of their territorial govern-ment. But since nonintervention was a policy applied only to southern territories (except in the Louisiana Purchase before 1820), the territorial decisions down until the late 1850s were invariably in favor of slavery. Thus, historically although not necessarily, nonintervention meant popular sovereignty, and popular sovereignty meant slavery.

The Missouri Compromise settled the issue of slavery in the territories for a generation. Many southerners looked back upon it with a strange ambivalence. The memory of the antislavery attack rankled; the 36° 30′ restriction embodied a demeaning and dangerous acknowledgment of congressional power. But at the same time, the concept of a dividing-line between free and slave territory carried an implication of sectional equality that never entirely lost its appeal in some southern eyes. Furthermore, as time passed, southerners tended increasingly to view the Compromise as an extraconstitutional settlement negotiated like a treaty between North and South in order to save the Union. As such, it implicitly exemplified Calhoun's principle of government by a concurrent majority.

The interval between the admission of Missouri and the introduction of the Wilmot Proviso was twenty-five years, almost to the day.[4] During those years, certain events and trends were shaping the crisis that David Wilmot precipitated on a sultry summer evening in 1846. In population, wealth, and industrial capacity, the South had fallen far behind the North and was much more conscious of its minority status than it had been a quarter of a century earlier. Yet, in the realm of politics, slaveholders were still the dominant social element in the government of the Republic.

The northern advantage in the House of Representatives had become greater than ever, it is true, but in the Senate there continued to be sectional parity. In fact, during the twenty-five years following the Missouri Compromise, three slave states and just one free state were admitted to the Union, and so on the day that Wilmot introduced his controversial Proviso, there were thirty southern senators and only twenty-six northern ones. The admission of Iowa later in 1846 and Wisconsin in 1848 restored the equilibrium.

Even more important to the South than its equal status in the Senate was the emergence of the second American party system. The bisectional strength of Whigs as well as Democrats meant that both parties had good reason to discountenance agitation of the slavery issue. Moreover, the Jacksonian Democrats—the stronger party of the two—were in many respects a resurrection of the Jeffersonian Republican organization that had served the South so well in its time. As the years passed, southern power and security came to depend more and more on southern dominance of the Democratic party.

Certainly the South in 1846 had many reasons to be pleased with its influence in national politics. The presidency continued to be in friendly hands. Southerners were still in the majority on the Supreme Court. Efforts to revive the national bank had failed, and tariff rates had been steadily reduced ever since the nullification crisis of 1832–1833.

Meanwhile, however, a new and uncommonly vehement challenge to southern security had emerged in the form of radical abolitionism, as personified by William Lloyd Garrison. There was a time when many historians regarded Garrison's launching of *The Liberator* on New Year's Day, 1831, as the opening gun of the Civil War. Albert J. Beveridge, working away on his biography of Lincoln in the 1920s, concluded that emancipation would have begun soon in the Border South had it not been for the Garrisonian crusade. "Darn those abolitionists," he wrote to Charles A. Beard. "The deeper I get into this thing, the clearer it becomes to me that the whole wretched mess could have been straightened out without the white race killing itself off, if the abolitionists had let matters alone."[5]

More recent scholarship has made it clear that the proslavery commitment of the South was well established before 1830 and therefore could not have originated as a response to the new antislavery radicalism. But if Garrisonian abolitionism was not the original cause of the sectional conflict over slavery, it nevertheless had a critical influence on the temper and shape of the conflict.

Out of passionate conviction, but also as a deliberate choice of strategy, the new abolitionists set out to destroy slavery by direct, personal attack upon everyone associated with the institution and everyone acquiescing in its existence. Their campaign of denunciation lacerated southern feelings as never before. The primary target, of course, was the slaveholder, whom they convicted of criminality, atrocity, and sin. Their language had the effect of degrading and dehumanizing the slaveholder, even as he was said to be degrading and dehumanizing his slaves.

The abolitionist crusade aggravated the southern fear that slave revolts could be inspired by northern agitation, and it evoked a related phenomenon of transcendent importance that perhaps can best be labeled "southern rage." By 1836, the crusade had turned Congress into a battleground over the receipt of abolitionist petitions and brought slavery to the center of national politics for the first time since the Missouri controversy.

To be sure, the abolitionists were highly unpopular in the North and constituted just a small fraction of the northern population. For the tactics of agitation, however, they were numerous enough to seem like an army, and their membership was heavily weighted with ministers, writers, editors, and other persons of more than average influence. Besides, the abolitionist movement was only part of a general antislavery trend that aroused apprehension and anger in the South. To understand fully the rage expressed by southerners like Robert Toombs during the crisis of 1846–1850, one must consider certain actions taken by northern state governments.

For example, Charles J. Faulkner of Virginia (later a congressman and minister to France) wrote to Calhoun in the summer of 1847 denouncing a piece of legislation as "the most deliberate and perfidious violation of all the guaranties of the

Constitution which the fanaticism and wickedness of the abolitionists have resorted to, and the most serious and dangerous attack yet made on the institution of slavery." Faulkner was talking, not about the Wilmot Proviso, as one might think, but rather about the personal liberty law recently enacted by the legislature of Pennsylvania. This measure, like others passed by northern states in the 1840s, was designed to protect free blacks from kidnapping, but it also impeded legitimate recovery of fugitive slaves. In addition, the new Pennsylvania law repealed a sojourning privilege dating back to 1788, whereby southerners could bring slaves into the state for visits of up to six months. Faulkner called the legislation of 1847 "a deliberate insult to the whole Southern people," which, among nations wholly independent, would be "a just cause for war." "Since the passage of this law," he wrote, "slaves are absconding from Maryland and this portion of Virginia in gangs of tens and twenties, and the moment they reach the Pennsylvania line all hopes of their recapture are abandoned."[6]

In respect to fugitive slaves, the South demanded not equality but special privilege of extraordinary proportions. Aside from the protection expected from the federal government, there was the right of private recapture, asserted and outlined by James M. Mason of Virginia on the Senate floor in January 1850. Under the fugitive-slave clause of the Constitution, said Mason, a slaveholder pursuing a fugitive into a free state had the right to enter any house without a warrant and seize an alleged slave by whatever force might be necessary. No person had a right to interfere with him or even to raise a question about the validity of his claim or the accuracy of his identification.[7] Thus the special privilege of the slaveholder took precedence over state sovereignty and civil liberty, even to the point of legalizing kidnapping. The fugitive-slave acts of 1793 and 1850 were both plainly unconstitutional if free Negroes came within the protection of the Fifth Amendment. There, indeed, was the essence of the dilemma. No law for the recovery of fugitive slaves could be effective without being outrageous. Yet southerners firmly believed that their right to an effective system of recovery was an article of solemn compact without which there could have been no Federal Union.

It appears that the number of slaves escaping into free states was relatively small—perhaps no more than a few hundred per year on the average. For southerners, however, the numbers were less important than the northern attitude and what it signified. "The loss of property is felt; the loss of honor is felt still more," Mason declared on a later occasion. "I say my people are degraded and humiliated when they are conscious that they tolerate a Government which is incapable of protecting them."[8] And when William H. Seward, during the debates of 1850, proposed a substitute bill guaranteeing accused fugitives the rights of habeas corpus and jury trial, there was this prompt and indignant response from Senator Henry S. Foote of Mississippi: "It cannot be that the American people have yet reached a depth of degradation so profound . . . as not to look upon this . . . attempt of the honorable Senator from New York to spoliate upon the . . . rights and interests of all the southern states . . . with pointed disapprobation, with hot contempt, with unmitigated loathing, and abhorrence unutterable."[9]

But the intensity of southern feeling on the subject is perhaps best indicated by the fact that the South Carolina Declaration of Causes of Secession, issued in December 1860, devoted twenty times as much space to the fugitive-slave problem as it did to the territorial question.[10]

Of course, the historical development most directly related to the crisis of 1846–1850 was the resumption of American territorial expansion after it had been in abeyance for a quarter of a century. The prospect of further expansion first arose in 1836 when the newly independent slaveholding Republic of Texas requested annexation to the United States. Fierce antislavery opposition greeted the proposal and helped delay annexation for nearly a decade. The Texas issue thus brought a militant antislavery movement into conflict with the new spirit of Manifest Destiny, exemplified in spread-eagle oratory and in wagons rolling westward to Oregon and California.

More than that, the Texas issue brought an enthusiastic expansionist named James K. Polk unexpectedly to the presidency and drove the United States predictably into hostilities with Mexico. Polk may or may not have been primarily responsible for starting the war, but he was certainly responsible for determining the *kind* of war it should be. His prompt dispatch of General Stephen W. Kearny to Santa Fe and Los Angeles indicated plainly enough that a war of territorial conquest had been set in motion. And so, just eight weeks after the declaration of war, David Wilmot introduced his famous Proviso.

The Wilmot Proviso was no fire bell in the night. It had been preceded by a decade of bitter sectional controversy in Congress over abolitionist petitions, slavery in the District of Columbia, and the annexation of Texas. The Proviso was sponsored, not by the most radical antislavery elements in Congress, but rather by a group of northern Democrats who had grown dissatisfied with southern domination of their party and with certain policies resulting from that domination. Some, for example, were angry about the recent presidential veto of a rivers-and-harbors appropriation, and some resented the Oregon Treaty signed with Great Britain in June. In each of these cases, the heavy hand of southern influence seemed all too visible. Polk's hostility to internal improvements at federal expense reflected the strict constructionism so dear to the Old South. As for Oregon, nearly half of it had been relinquished after the great expanse of Texas had been secured for slaveholders, and now southerners presumably expected to obtain still more slave territory as a prize of war. The Proviso, in the circumstances, seemed an appropriate retaliation. It forbade slavery in any territory that might be acquired from Mexico.

Here was a proposal so radical that it had no real precedent except perhaps Jefferson's abortive effort in 1784 to prohibit slavery throughout the trans-Appalachian West. Its full import did not become clear until the Treaty of Guadalupe Hidalgo in 1848 confirmed the cession of the Southwest to the United States. The Proviso, taken together with the general assumption that Oregon was bound to be free territory, would mean the exclusion of slavery from the entire American Far West, an area as large as the Louisiana Purchase. Compounding the outrageousness of the proposal, in southern eyes, was the fact that the land conquered from Mexico had cost lives as well as money. It had been purchased, the phrase ran, "by the blood and treasure" of the whole nation; yet half the nation was to be excluded from its benefits.

The Proviso itself would not have shocked the South and precipitated a sectional crisis if it had not received such overwhelming northern support in Congress and so much vehement endorsement in northern editorials, northern legislative resolutions, and northern party conventions. "The madmen of the North," said the Richmond *Enquirer*, ". . . have, we fear, cast the die, and numbered the days of this glorious Union." [11] The view that the southern states must secede if the Proviso should be enacted was probably more widespread in the South than the view in 1860 that the election of Lincoln would make secession necessary. Even Alexander H. Stephens said so. "The day in which aggression is consummated upon any section of the country . . . this Union is dissolved," he declared. "I would rather that the southern country should perish—that all her statesmen and all her gallant spirits should be buried in honorable graves—than submit for one instant to degradation." [12]

But the Proviso, although approved a number of times in the House of Representatives, never really had a chance of passing the Senate. Because of the nature of the crisis—because the crisis had been created in Congress and could be dissolved in Congress—the course of events was running through much passionate oratory toward another sectional compromise.

The struggle over the Wilmot Proviso resembled the Missouri controversy in a number of ways, but there were also some important differences between them. For one thing, the primary issue in 1819–1820 had been the admission of a slave state (Missouri), with the territorial question remaining secondary; whereas, in 1846–1850, the primary issue from the beginning was slavery in the territories, with admission of a free state (California) arising as a related but secondary matter.

As a consequence, the lines of argument were considerably different in the crisis of 1846–1850. For instance, the South, in order to defend its rights in the territories while adhering faithfully to the doctrine of state sovereignty, had to rely heavily upon what Arthur Bestor calls the principle of "extrajurisdictional" power—which meant, in effect, that a slaveholder entering federal territory, like a slaveholder pursuing a fugitive slave into another state, took with him the law of his own state and its protective force.[13]

Another difference between the two crises was that slavery had been legal under the preceding regime in Louisiana but illegal under the preceding regime in the Mexican Cession. Antislavery spokesmen could therefore argue that the equivalent of the Wilmot Proviso had been inherited from Mexico and would remain in force until superseded by American law. The argument, if valid, converted nonintervention, which had always been functionally permissive of slavery, into silent confirmation of a ban on slavery in the Southwest.

In response to this challenge, southerners elaborated and perfected the "common-property" doctrine—usually associated with resolutions introduced by Calhoun in 1847, although it had come into use some time before. Congress, according to the

Calhoun theory, was merely the "joint-agent" of the sovereign states and, as such, had no power to prevent the citizens of any states from "emigrating with their property" (meaning slaves) into the territories, which were not the property of the federal government, but rather the "common property" of the states. Slaveholding in the territories was therefore a right protected by the *direct force* of the Constitution, which superseded Mexican law in the Southwest and at the same time prevented Congress from enacting any such measure as the Wilmot Proviso.[14]

But of course the Constitution *has* no force until it is applied by some agency, and so the common-property doctrine, however appropriate it might be as an *answer* to the Proviso, was not a functional *alternative* to the Proviso. It was a theory of right and power but not a design of public policy. As a matter of policy, many southerners who embraced the common-property doctrine were prepared to advocate, or at least to accept, extension of the Missouri Compromise line to the Pacific. This involved them in the glaring inconsistency of denying the power of Congress to enact the Wilmot Proviso while acknowledging that same power if it were exercised only north of 36° 30′. Their explanation was that, in order to save the Union, they were willing to go beyond the restraints of the Constitution, though not beyond the principles of justice.

Extension of the Missouri Compromise line soon proved to be useless as a basis for compromise, however. Early in 1847, an effort to attach it by implication to a bill organizing Oregon Territory failed in the House of Representatives, 82 to 113, with only six northerners voting in the affirmative. Another such attempt the following year was defeated even more decisively, and Oregon, after two years of waiting, was finally organized as a free territory without reference to the rest of the Far West.[15]

Thus, a striking reversal had taken place. In 1820, the Missouri Compromise line had been a concession made to the

North as part of the price for the admission of Missouri as a slave state, and nearly half of the southern representatives had opposed it. In 1846–1847, extension of the line was demanded by southerners as the price for organization of Oregon as a free territory, and nearly all of the northern representatives opposed it. One reason for the change, as southerners resentfully noted, was that much more of the land at stake in 1846 lay south of 36° 30′.

As it became increasingly plain that extension of the 36° 30′ line would never win acceptance, opponents of the Wilmot Proviso began to look for a more acceptable formula of compromise. One measure, sponsored unsuccessfully by John M. Clayton of Delaware in 1848, would have left the status of slavery in the Mexican Cession to judicial determination. Later that year, Stephen A. Douglas proposed that Congress admit the entire Southwest directly to statehood, thus bypassing the territorial stage and avoiding the convulsive territorial issue.[16]

Most important of all, however, was the solution brought forward by several northern Democrats and given the name "popular sovereignty." Congress, they maintained, could not, or at least should not, interfere with slavery in the territories and instead must leave the problem entirely to the decision of the territorial population. This doctrine, though offered as new theory, in fact recapitulated old practice. It described the policy established by Congress in 1790 for territory south of the Ohio River and reaffirmed in 1820 for that part of the Louisiana Purchase lying south of 36° 30′. Southerners in those earlier years of the Republic had not needed or asked for anything more— had not demanded positive federal laws protecting slavery in southern territories. But patterns of migration were changing in the 1840s, and the old policy of nonintervention could no longer be regarded as safely proslavery in its effect. Besides, the advocates of popular sovereignty like Douglas and Lewis Cass, in trying to sell the doctrine to their northern constituencies, laid heavy emphasis upon the power of territorial governments to prohibit slavery. And sometimes they added in stage whispers that, since nature had made the Southwest inhospitable to slavery, popular sovereignty would have the same effect there as the Wilmot Proviso, without giving mortal offense to the South.

Such argument did not encourage southern support, and the South, in fact, never developed much enthusiasm for the Cass-Douglas version of popular sovereignty. Yet, certain ambiguities in the doctrine made it useful to the Democratic party as a means of moderating and concealing internal sectional quarrels over slavery, especially in presidential election years. Northern Democrats and southern Democrats could talk about popular sovereignty (or nonintervention) and have different things in mind. This dissimulation was a frail vessel of party unity, but it stayed afloat until 1857, when the Supreme Court blew it out of the water.

When the Thirty-first Congress convened in December 1849, nearly two years after the Treaty of Guadalupe Hidalgo, the newly acquired Southwest was still without territorial organization, and the sectional crisis had reached its peak. The Gold Rush made California's need for stable government more urgent every day. The extravagant boundary claims of Texas seemed likely to produce violence in the Santa Fe region. Nearly all northern legislatures had passed resolutions endorsing the principle of the Wilmot Proviso. And southerners were becoming more and more convinced that in Zachary Taylor the nation had elected a reverse doughface—that is, a southern man with northern principles—to the presidency.

Taylor, who had fallen under the antislavery influence of William H. Seward and had said publicly that there would be no further extension of slavery, adopted as administration policy the old Douglas scheme of bypassing the territorial issue by admitting California and New Mexico directly to statehood.

Californians, with presidential encouragement but no authorization from Congress, proceeded to draft a constitution, establish a state government, and ask for admission to the Union as a free state.

The purpose of the Wilmot Proviso was about to be achieved by indirection, or so it appeared to outraged southerners. Any men of the South who would "consent to be thus degraded and enslaved," said Thomas L. Clingman of North Carolina, "ought to be whipped through their fields by their own negroes." [17] And Alexander H. Stephens, determined to resist "the dictation of Northern hordes of Goths and Vandals," suggested that southern states should be "making the necessary preparations of men and money, arms and munitions, etc., to meet the emergency." [18] The sense of emergency strengthened the movement toward southern unity, which culminated in an ominous call from Mississippi for a convention to meet in Nashville on the first Monday in June 1850. Our retrospective knowledge of what happened in 1850—especially Taylor's death and how it cleared the way for compromise—makes it extremely difficult for us to understand how desperate the situation seemed in the winter of 1849–1850.

Achievement of the Compromise of 1850 is one of the greatest legislative and oratorical events in American history, complete with moments of high drama, such as Calhoun's brooding valedictory presented just twenty-seven days before his death. The central issue was whether California should be admitted as a free state *with* or *without* accompanying concessions to the South in the rest of the Mexican Cession. But there were other problems also requiring attention, and Henry Clay provided a formula of general compromise in a set of resolutions introduced in the Senate on January 29. [19]

From that beginning, the familiar story line runs through the creation of a select Committee of Thirteen in April; the construction of the famous "Omnibus Bill" in May; Taylor's death and the destruction of the Omnibus in July; and then, between July 31 and September 17, passage of the Compromise as six separate measures in the Senate and five in the House of Representatives (where two bills were joined together for strategic reasons). The Compromise included the admission of California, organization of Utah and New Mexico territories without restrictions on slavery, reduction of the area of Texas, federal assumption of the Texas debt, prohibition of the domestic slave trade in the District of Columbia, and a more stringent fugitive-slave law.

All of the measures passed easily in the Senate. There was more resistance, as expected, at the other end of the Capitol. But the House, like its counterpart of thirty years earlier, ended by retreating from the position that it had held for so long and with such tenacity. In yielding to the strong pressure for compromise that had been built up during the many months of senatorial debate, the House not only surrendered the Proviso principle twice but also passed the provocative Fugitive Slave Act by a comfortable margin. All in all, it was a remarkable collapse of antislavery strength.

Only four senators and twenty-eight representatives voted for *all* the compromise measures. This is probably too strict a criterion to be useful, however; for a good many true supporters of compromise (like Douglas and Thomas Hart Benton) missed one or more of the final votes. If we define a supporter of the Compromise as someone who voted for at least four of the five measures related to the slavery question, and who opposed none of the five, the totals rise to fourteen in the Senate and forty-seven in the House. Of these sixty-one compromisers (constituting about 21 percent of the entire congressional membership), thirty-eight were northern Democrats, and eleven were southern Whigs—the two political groups that suffered most severely from the strains of party and sectional cross-pressures.[20]

Fifty-seven of the sixty-one, including thirteen from the Border South, represented states that did not leave the Union in 1860–1861. The eleven states of the Confederate South, whose total representation exceeded ninety, contributed only four compromisers, and there were none at all from South Carolina, Mississippi, Florida, Alabama, Georgia, and Louisiana—the first six states to secede in 1860–1861. Remember, if you will, how different it had been in 1820, when *northern* members of Congress were the ones overwhelmingly against the Compromise and the Lower South was relatively amenable to it.

In 1820, southerners had been forced to pay for the admission of Missouri as the only slave state extending north of the fortieth parallel. The payment was *prohibition* of slavery in the rest of the Louisiana Purchase lying north of 36° 30′. In 1850, northerners were made to pay for the admission of California as the first free state to extend south of the thirty-seventh parallel. The payment was *permission* of slavery in the rest of the Far West lying south of 42°.

If our conception of the Compromise of 1850 is expanded, as it should be, to include the organization of Oregon Territory in 1848 with slavery forbidden, it then becomes plain that the old policy of having two policies was continued. Unable to secure the extension of the Missouri Compromise line to the Pacific, the South, in effect, traded off the loss of southern California for the opening of Utah to slavery. As a consequence, the dividing-line, which had been first the Ohio River and then 36° 30′ (except for Missouri), became 42° in the Far West (except for California). North of the 42° dividing-line, slavery was prohibited in federal territory; south of the line, slavery was permitted in federal territory, just as had been the case ever since 1790. Stephens understood all of this very well. Replying to a critic back in Georgia who complained that he should have continued to support 36° 30′, he asked:

Do you mean the extension of the provisions of the Missouri Compromise, by which slavery was forever prohibited *north* of that line, leaving the people *south* of it to do as they pleased upon the subject of slavery? If so, was it not much better for the.South . . . to let the people do as they pleased over the whole territory up to 42 deg. north latitude, just as the Utah and New Mexican bills, which passed, provide, than to have the people *restricted* in any portion of the territory?[21]

Yet, for many Americans, 36° 30′ had come to have a magical quality, and they regarded any policy without it as an abandonment of the entire dividing-line principle. Douglas, who spoke erroneously of 36° 30′ as a dividing-line between freedom and *slavery*, seems never to have perceived that the territorial legislation of 1848–1850 continued a policy of dividing the West between freedom and *nonintervention*. Viewing the Utah and New Mexico acts without reference to Oregon, he saw them as introducing a new compromise principle—popular sovereignty—to replace the dividing-line policy. This misconception, with which he rationalized his sponsorship of the Kansas-Nebraska bill in 1854, has been perpetuated by a number of historians, most notably, perhaps, by Robert R. Russel in an influential article entitled "What Was the Compromise of 1850?"[22]

The Utah and New Mexico legislation did not constitute a compromise in itself, with "mutual concessions," as Russel maintains, and it did not install the Cass-Douglas version of popular sovereignty as official policy. Rather, the legislation constituted a victory for the South, offsetting the admission of California; for it rejected the Wilmot Proviso and embodied the principle of nonintervention, from which the Calhoun property-rights doctrine could be inferred, just as well as popular sovereignty. Russel concludes that it would be "futile to attempt to say which side came off the better" in the territorial legislation of 1850, but the members of Congress seem to have made the judgment readily enough. Eighty-two percent of the southerners in both houses voted for the Utah bill, and 62 percent of the northerners voted against it.

To have defeated the Proviso and secured passage of the first fugitive-slave law in over fifty years was no mean achievement for southern statesmanship. Acquiescence in the Compromise accordingly prevailed throughout the South, but not without a hard struggle in some states. The eventual triumph of Unionism everywhere is perhaps less significant than the fact that a sizable part of the electorate in South Carolina, Georgia, Alabama, and Mississippi continued to lean toward disunion even after the Compromise had been passed.[23]

Moreover, the Unionism that triumphed in the Lower South and Middle South was predominantly "conditional" Unionism —which is to say, conditional *dis*unionism. For, phrased either way, the concept meant: Under some conditions we will remain in the Union, and under other conditions we will not. The view of secession as a legal right probably gained considerable ground during the crisis. Howell Cobb, fighting Georgia secessionists in his famous campaign for governor in 1851, was one of those "Unionists" who found it wise to straddle the issue. The Federal Union was intended by its founders to be perpetual, he declared, and a state had no constitutional right to secede—except for just cause, to be determined by the state herself.[24]

Just as the Slaveholding South by 1820 had committed itself to the permanency of slavery, even while continuing to label the institution an evil, so the Confederate South by 1850 had embraced the principle of secessionism, even while rejecting immediate secession.[25] The Compromise legislation of 1850, though apparently resolving a number of vexatious and even dangerous problems, had scarcely touched the deeper, ineluctable conflict over slavery. The effect was to defuse the accumulated charge of sectional hostility without dismantling it. After so many stormy months of crisis, nearly everyone welcomed the period of relative calm that followed; but it was, in the words of one southern editor, "the calm of preparation, and not of peace."[26]

3 Kansas, Republicanism, and the Crisis of the Union

"All Christendom is leagued against the South upon this question of domestic slavery," said James Buchanan on the Senate floor in 1842. "They have no other allies to sustain their constitutional rights, except the Democracy of the North. . . . In my own State, we inscribe upon our banners hostility to abolition. It is there one of the cardinal principles of the Democratic party." [1]

The crisis of 1850 once again confirmed the crucial importance of northern Democrats in the southern strategy of defense, and it also revealed the extent to which that defense might be breached by an unsympathetic president. The South accordingly appears to have benefited more from the political consequences of the Compromise of 1850 than from any of its specific provisions. For a reunited Democratic party, pledging faithful adherence to the Compromise, swept to victory in the presidential election of 1852 and also won a two-thirds majority in the House of Representatives.

During the next eight years, under Franklin Pierce and his successor, James Buchanan, southern influence dominated the executive branch of the federal government through the agency of northern doughfaces like Caleb Cushing and Jeremiah S.

Black, as well as southerners like Jefferson Davis and Howell Cobb. Throughout the period, the Senate remained safely Democratic and therefore safely prosouthern on slavery questions. In the House of Representatives, three of the five speakers serving between 1850 and 1860 were Democrats from Georgia, Kentucky, and South Carolina. Seven of the nine members of the Supreme Court were Democrats; and in 1857, six of them declared the Missouri Compromise restriction unconstitutional on the ground that Congress had no power to prohibit slavery in the territories.

Of course, these were things that southerners had come to expect. In 1861, Alexander H. Stephens reminded his fellow Georgians: "We have had a majority of the Presidents chosen from the South; as well as the control and management of most of those chosen from the North." Then he went on to name other offices in which southerners had outnumbered northerners: Supreme Court justices, 18 to 11; speakers of the House, 23 to 12; presidents pro tem of the Senate, 24 to 11; attorneys general, 14 to 5; foreign ministers, 86 to 54; and in the appointment of some 3,000 clerks, auditors, and controllers, better than a two-to-one advantage.[2]

The extraordinary power traditionally exercised by southerners in national affairs constituted one of the principal deterrents to disunion; for as long as it endured, the South had better reason to remain in the Union than to leave. It was the loss of a substantial part of that power in 1860 that drove the seven states of the Lower South into secession, and the critical element in the loss was the weakened condition of the South's only ally in Christendom—the northern Democracy.

The structure of southern power in national politics during the 1850s was a kind of holding-company arrangement in which the South held majority control of the Democratic party, and the Democrats were the majority party in the nation. The same pattern had prevailed during much of the preceding half century, and the recent experience with Zachary Taylor had revealed that the Whig party could *not* be brought under southern control—not even when it was headed by a southern slaveholder. In any case, the distress of the Whig party soon left the Democrats as the only national party organization through which the South could exercise national power.

Nothing, then, was more vital to southern security within the Union than maintaining the majority status of the Democratic party. And in this respect, the Democratic victory in 1852 was not as overwhelming as it appeared on the surface, especially in the North. Although Pierce carried fourteen out of the sixteen free states, he did so with only a plurality of their popular vote. The structure of southern political power therefore resembled a bridge that rested at one end on an insecure foundation. To be sure, Democratic mastery seemed firm enough in 1853, with the presidency recaptured and the party controlling both houses of the incoming Congress by huge majorities. But this flush of prosperity proved to be ominous, in a way, and also treacherous —ominous because of what it signified about the condition of the Whig party, and treacherous because it encouraged the disastrous blunder of the Kansas-Nebraska Act.

The disintegration of the Whig party, and thus of the second American party system, began with the alienation of southern Whigs from Taylor in 1849–1850 and was largely completed by 1855. Historians continue to ponder the question of why the Whig party perished in the 1850s while the Democratic party, though presumably subject to the same disruptive pressures, managed to survive. It may be, simply, that the Whigs lacked the symbolic appeal, the tradition of victory, and the degree of cohesion necessary for survival in the 1850s. Another explanation is that Whiggery was in a sense absorbed by the burgeoning nativist movement, which then failed in *its* efforts to become a major, bisectional party. But in addition, it appears that differences of sectional balance *within* the two parties may account for the greater vulnerability of the Whigs. Since the South was much more united than the North on the issue of slavery, it was accordingly easier for many northern Democrats to remain within a party increasingly dominated by proslavery southerners than it was for southern Whigs to remain within a party increasingly dominated by antislavery northerners. That is probably why the disruption of the second American party system started with the collapse of Whiggery in several states of the Lower South.[3]

Why the Whig organization did not at least survive in the North as a major antislavery party, instead of giving way to the Republicans, is another question and need not be answered here.[4] The point is that the death of the Whig party as a national organization proved harmful to the health of the Democratic party and thus to the structure of southern political power. For the Democrats, during the later 1850s, were opposed in both the North and the South by sectional or local parties that did not have to make any concessions to intersectional accommodation within their organizations. The cross-pressures of party and section upon northern Democrats became much more severe when the Whigs were replaced by a more aggressively antislavery party that stood to profit organizationally from continued agitation of the slavery issue. The challenge of Republicanism compelled men like Stephen A. Douglas, in the interest of political survival, to show more independence of southern influence where slavery was concerned, and this necessity could not fail to place heavy strains upon party unity.

And even in the South, where the Democrats themselves were supposedly the radical party on sectional issues, they came under cross-pressure from the post-Whig opposition parties, which, as a matter of political strategy, often tried to outdo them in proslavery extremism. It was the southern opposition press, for instance, that started the attacks on Buchanan's Kansas policy in the summer of 1857, and it was the southern opposition press that set up the loudest clamor for a territorial slave code two years later. As John V. Mering has pointed out, "Only in Tennessee among southern states that had elections for governor in 1859 did the Opposition refrain from taking a stronger stand on behalf of slavery in the territories than the Democrats." [5]

But the first baneful consequence of the Whig decline was passage of the Kansas-Nebraska bill, which never could have been accomplished if the Democrats had not held such large majorities in both houses of Congress. The bill received the support of nearly nine-tenths of all southern members casting votes and nearly three-fourths of all Democrats. It was an official party measure, endorsed and vigorously promoted by the Pierce administration, but its disruptive influence is strikingly illustrated by the fact that in the House of Representatives, northern Democrats were divided, 44 in favor and 44 against. [6] The political aftermath turned into a Democratic nightmare, with waves of popular indignation sweeping through the free states, 66 out of 91 House seats held by northern Democrats lost in the midterm elections, and the emergence of a broad anti-Nebraska coalition that would soon crystallize into the Republican party.

The struggle over the Kansas-Nebraska bill was the most egregious of several instances in which southerners, during the 1850s, traded some of their power advantage for empty sectional victories. Although its momentous consequences are plain to see, the struggle is of interest not only because of what it did *to* the South, but also because of what it revealed *about* the South.

Historians differ about the degree to which southerners of the 1850s were committed to the further expansion of slavery. The South delineated by William L. Barney, for instance, was a society in constant need of more room for its growing slave population and of new land to replace its easily depleted soils. "The continual maturation of slavery within a fixed geographical area," he writes, "created class and racial stresses that could be relieved only through expansion." Furthermore, "as long as the option of adding slave territory was kept open, Southerners could delude themselves with the comforting belief that eventually slavery and its terrible racial dilemma could vanish slowly and painlessly, by a diffusion of all the blacks out of the American South into the tropics of Central and South America."[7]

On the other hand, there are historians disposed to believe that the sectional controversy of the 1850s had less to do with the further expansion of slavery than with the future of slavery in modern America. In their view, the pernicious and seemingly useless quarrel over the territories was primarily a symbolic struggle laden with implication—or, as has been said, "merely the skirmish line of a larger and more fundamental conflict."[8]

No doubt there is room enough for both interpretations in any comprehensive explanation of the coming of the Civil War, but southern expansionism hardly seems to have been the animating spirit of the Kansas-Nebraska Act. The measure, by repealing the 36° 30' restriction of the Missouri Compromise, admitted slavery into an area unsuited for it and in no way facilitated the expansion of slavery southward into areas that *were* suited for it.

It is true that some southerners cherished the hope of making Kansas the sixteenth slave state, but even if they had succeeded, it would have been a nominal and temporary triumph gained at excessive cost. Proslavery imperialism became an absurdity in Kansas, and, as far as southern political power was concerned, it would have been much better strategy to settle for the admission of Kansas as a free but *Democratic* state, like the three states actually admitted in the 1850s—California, Minnesota, and Oregon. That was precisely the strategy adopted by Robert J. Walker as governor of Kansas in 1857, but the South rose up in revolt against it and saw Kansas admitted just a few years later as a Republican state instead.

The bitterest irony in the Kansas-Nebraska Act was that its sponsors justified it as a logical and reconciliatory extension of the Compromise of 1850. They insisted, erroneously, that the old dividing-line policy had been replaced with a new, uniform national policy of nonintervention and that, accordingly, to retain the slavery restriction north of 36° 30′ in the organization of new territories would violate the letter and spirit of the recent Compromise. Actually, however, the popularity of the Compromise of 1850 resulted largely from its general pacificatory effect, not from any principles that could be inferred from its specific provisions. In short, the clearest violation of the spirit of the Compromise would be *any* legislative action that revived the slavery controversy. And the political power of the South, depending as it did upon the strength and unity of the Democratic party, likewise stood to suffer grievously from any renewal of slavery agitation. Southerners must have realized as well as Douglas that repeal of the Missouri Compromise restriction would, in his words, "raise a hell of a storm." Why, then, did they risk so much for so little to be gained?

For one thing, it appears that the southern members of Congress more or less drifted into the Kansas-Nebraska struggle without giving it much thought beforehand. Certainly there was no strong pressure on them from home to secure the repeal at that time, and it is notable that members from the Lower South were not prominent in the early stages of the affair. In fact, the senator who initiated the move to make the repeal explicit was a Kentucky Whig—the successor of Henry Clay.

Southern press support for the Kansas-Nebraska bill was relatively restrained, as Avery O. Craven has shown. "It is difficult for us to comprehend, or credit the excitement . . . in the North on account of the Nebraska question," wrote an Alabaman in the summer of 1854. "Here," he continued, "there is no excitement, no fever, on the subject. It is seldom alluded to in private or public and so far as the introduction of slavery

[into Kansas and Nebraska] is concerned, such a consumma-
tion is hardly hoped for."[9] But the savage northern denunciation of the measure encouraged southern members to close
ranks on the issue, and they supplied more than 60 percent of
the votes cast for passage. With sectional violence thereafter
erupting and becoming chronic on the prairies of Kansas, the
South's emotional investment in the proslavery cause in Kansas
grew to enormous proportions, even while the chances of gain-
ing anything of.practical importance were steadily dwindling.

Southern attitudes throughout the Kansas controversy demonstrate the intensely reactive nature of southern sectionalism.
That is, the South did not so much respond to the Kansas-
Nebraska issue itself as react to the northern response to the
issue; and much the same thing happened four years later in the
struggle over the Lecompton constitution. Similarly, what an-
gered southerners most about John Brown's raid on Harpers
Ferry was the amount of applause it received in the North.

The language of antislavery denunciation had a cumulative
effect by the 1850s, and southern skin, far from toughening
under attack, had become increasingly sensitive. According to
Senator Judah P. Benjamin of Louisiana, the heart of the matter was not so much what the abolitionists and Republicans had
done or might *do* to the South, as it was "the things they *said*"
about the South—and the moral arrogance with which they
said them.[10] Southerners, though often emphatically denying
it, in fact cared deeply about northern opinion of the South and
its people. They wanted, above all, an end to being treated as
moral inferiors, and thus an end to the fear of eventually *accepting* the badge of inferiority. The result, says Charles G. Sellers,
was a "series of constantly mounting demands for symbolic acts
by which the North would say that slavery was all right."[11]

The most conspicuous badge of sectional inferiority was overt
federal prohibition of slavery in the territories. For many southerners by the 1850s, such exclusion had become a moral re-

proach of unbearable weight. When Douglas offered them the opportunity to erase a large part of the stigma by repealing the Missouri Compromise restriction, they could scarcely do otherwise than grasp it.

The symbolic victory thus achieved in the Kansas-Nebraska Act was not really expected to bring any tangible benefits. But the course of events in Kansas did conspire to offer the South a chance in 1858 to win another victory of the same kind—that is, the admission of Kansas as a nominal slaveholding state under the Lecompton constitution. Once again, and in an even more dubious cause, southern members of Congress closed ranks. Knowing that the constitution did not represent the will of the territorial population, knowing that Kansas was destined to be a free state whatever the formal terms of her admission might be, and knowing that the issue would surely cause havoc among the northern Democracy, they nevertheless voted almost unanimously for the Lecompton bill.[12]

Again there appeared to be an important principle at stake. For here was an opportunity to test one of the items in the Georgia platform of 1850—namely, whether a slave state could ever again be admitted to the Union, now that an antislavery party had become predominant in the North. There had *been* no such admission, after all, since that of Texas twelve years earlier. The test came, moreover, in the aftermath of the Dred Scott decision, when southerners were again reacting to a northern reaction and also discarding the notion that the Constitution, of its own force, gave them any protection against antislavery attack.

As it became increasingly clear that the Lecompton bill, with half of the northern Democrats opposing it, could not command a majority in the House, another secession crisis developed. The ultimatum "Lecompton or disunion" reverberated in the halls of Congress, in the southern press, and in southern legislatures. With Alabama leading the way, contingent steps toward secession were officially taken by several states. "Upon the action of this Congress, must depend the union or disunion of this great Confederacy," a Georgia congressman warned. The people of the South were determined, he said, "to have equality in this Union or independence out of it . . . you must admit Kansas . . . with the Lecompton constitution." [13] "The equilibrium in the balance of power is already lost," declared a member from Mississippi. "Reject Kansas and the cordon is then completed. . . . Against this final act of degradation I believe the South will resist—resist with arms." [14] "Save the Union, if you can," wrote a South Carolinian to Senator James H. Hammond. "But rather than have Kansas refused admission under the Lecompton Constitution, let it perish in blood and fire." [15]

The symbolic importance of the issue was not diminished but rather was enhanced by the fact that the South had nothing material to gain from the admission. As Buchanan's pro-Lecompton message to Congress perceptively argued: "In considering this question, it should never be forgotten that in proportion to its insignificance . . . the rejection of the constitution will be so much the more keenly felt by the people of . . . the States of this Union, where slavery is recognized." [16] So, paradoxically, the very futility of the proslavery cause in Kansas made the Lecompton question more clearly a "point of honor" and a meaningful test of how *little* could be expected from the North in the way of concessions. In the words of one South Carolinian, it would have been "dirt cheap" for the free states to yield. [17]

Once again, however, a legislative crisis ended in a legislative compromise—or rather, in this case, a pseudocompromise that did not conceal the reality of southern defeat. The critical question was whether the Lecompton bill should be passed as it was or be amended to allow resubmission of the constitution to the voters of Kansas, which would surely mean rejection. With the House of Representatives this time standing its ground, southern members of Congress ended by accepting the so-called "English compromise," which provided for an indirect resubmission of the constitution and thus allowed them to save face a little with their constituents.

For this miserable achievement the South paid dearly. The Democratic party, split by an anti-Lecompton revolt with Douglas at its head, suffered another election defeat in 1858 and became the minority party in virtually every northern state. From that point on, the odds favored election of a Republican president in 1860. Moreover, the English compromise was so obviously a southern backdown from the threat of disunion that it encouraged Republicans to regard later secession threats as mere resumption of a game of bluff.

The compromise nevertheless satisfied many southerners, even some aiming at disunion, because it enabled them to retreat from a shaky limb. The Lecompton constitution, for a number of reasons, provided a very dubious basis for a sectional ultimatum. Governor Joseph E. Brown of Georgia, who was ready at the time to inaugurate a secession movement, later acknowledged that an outright defeat of the Lecompton bill would have caused "great confusion," and that "the democratic party of the state would have been divided and distracted."[18] It appears, then, that in 1858 there was some possibility of an *unsuccessful* secession movement that might have thrown secessionism generally into disrepute and thus, like a small earthquake, taken off some of the underlying stress.

The Lecompton affair proved to be the last full-dress legislative crisis and compromise in the tradition of 1819–1821, 1832–1833, and 1846–1850. Reflecting upon the pattern of events from the introduction of the Tallmadge proviso to the hollow triumph of the English compromise, one is disposed to doubt that legislative crisis was ever the proper fuse for setting off a civil war in the United States. A crisis arising in Congress could usually be controlled by Congress. The greatest danger in 1850, for instance, had been that presidential intervention might take matters out of congressional hands.

The end of the Lecompton controversy in fact marked the end of the territorial issue as a serious threat to the Union. Kansas ceased to be disputed ground and was admitted quietly as a free state in 1861. There was no other sectional issue with which Congress seemed likely, in the near future, to create another legislative crisis. Certainly not the agitation for a reopening of the African slave trade; for that had only minority support even in the Lower South. And certainly not the issue of a slave code for the territories, which provoked so much congressional debate in 1859 and 1860. That was not a southern demand upon Congress for legislation, but rather a southern Democratic demand upon Douglas for renunciation of his apostasy or withdrawal from the approaching presidential race.

James Buchanan had entered the presidency in 1857 determined to end the conflict in Kansas and thereby restore sectional peace. He hoped that "geographical parties," as he phrased it in his inaugural, would then "speedily become extinct." [19] His efforts ended in a curious mixture of success and failure; for the resolution of the Kansas problem, by the very manner in which it was accomplished, substantially increased the strength of the Republican party.

The disintegration of the Whig party, and hence the breakup of the second American party system, had begun before 1854, but it was the Kansas-Nebraska Act, more than anything else, that determined the character of the third party system in its early years. If the sectional truce of 1850 had remained more or less in effect, the Whig party might well have been succeeded by the Native American or Know-Nothing party. Instead, with the slavery controversy reopened to the point of violence, the anti-

Nebraska coalition of 1854 swiftly converted itself into the nation's first major party organized on antislavery principles. Suddenly, the South faced a new menace and a new potential cause for secession—the possibility that a Republican might be elected to the presidency.

The causes for secession listed in the Georgia platform of 1850, it will be remembered, had all been legislative acts that might be passed by Congress.[20] The sectional crises of 1820, 1833, 1850, and 1858 had all been precipitated by such legislation, enacted or proposed. But, beginning in 1856, the election of a Republican president became a more probable occasion for disunion than any legislative proposal likely to receive serious consideration in Congress. Beginning in 1856, a different finger was on the trigger mechanism. Control passed from the professional politician to the ordinary voter, particularly the northern voter. And if worse should come to worst, how did one go about compromising the results of a presidential election?

It was difficult for the people of the South to view Republicans as merely a political opposition. "If they should succeed in this contest," said a North Carolina newspaper in September 1856, "the result will be a separation of the States. No human power can prevent it. . . . They would create insurrection and servile war in the South—they would put the torch to our dwellings and the knife to our throats. They are, therefore, our enemies."[21]

We should perhaps pay more attention to the fact that 1856 was a year of genuine secession crisis, mitigated only by the general belief that the Republicans had but an outside chance of capturing the presidency. For southerners, the outcome of the election spelled temporary relief but very little reassurance. The Democrats did elect James Buchanan to succeed Franklin Pierce, and they did recapture control of the House of Representatives. Buchanan triumphed by sweeping the South, except for Maryland, and by carrying also the five free states of New Jersey, Pennsylvania, Indiana, Illinois, and California. But only two of those five states gave him popular majorities—Indiana, 50.4 percent, and his own Pennsylvania, 50.1 percent. The Democratic share of the free-state vote fell from 50.7 percent in 1852 to 41.4 percent in 1856. John C. Frémont, the Republican candidate, outpolled Buchanan in the North by more than a hundred thousand votes. Frémont and Millard Fillmore, the American party candidate, together outpolled him by more than a half million votes in the North. There was little difficulty visualizing what would happen to the Democratic party in the free states if its divided opposition should become united. The party had, in fact, hung on to the presidency with its fingertips; and the loss of that precarious hold, even many conservative southerners agreed, would mean a prompt disruption of the Union.

In these circumstances, the all-out drive to make Kansas a slave state under the Lecompton constitution was plain political folly. And the midterm congressional elections of 1858 accordingly proved disastrous for the Democrats because of what happened in those same northern states that Buchanan had carried two years earlier. The Republicans increased their share of the total vote in New Jersey, Pennsylvania, Indiana, and Illinois from 35 percent in 1856 to 52 percent in 1858. The most stunning reversal came in Pennsylvania. There, just the year before, the Democrats had elected a governor by more than forty thousand votes, but in 1858 they lost nearly all of their congressional seats and were outpolled by twenty-five thousand votes. "We have met the enemy in Pennsylvania," said Buchanan, "and we are theirs."[22]

From the Lecompton struggle onward, all the signs of the times pointed to a Republican victory in 1860 and to some kind of secession movement as a consequence. Yet the Democratic party, instead of reuniting to meet the danger, became increasingly a house divided against itself. The quarrel between Douglas and the South, aside from its strong influence on the shape of the final crisis, deserves attention because of what it reveals about the psychological escalation of the sectional conflict.

Douglas in 1856 had been the favorite presidential nominee of the South, and especially of the Lower South, which gave him thirty-eight of its forty-seven votes at the Cincinnati convention. Four years later at Charleston, however, delegates from the Lower South walked out of the convention rather than accept his leadership of the party. In the interval, Douglas made his fight against the Lecompton constitution, opposing even the English compromise; he issued the Freeport doctrine during the debates with Lincoln as a means of salvaging the principle of popular sovereignty while at the same time endorsing the Dred Scott decision; and, presumably as a consequence of those actions, he managed to win reelection to the Senate against the Republican tide that swept so many northern Democrats out of office in 1858.

It was success at the polls that the South needed most from its northern allies, but what southern Democratic leaders proceeded to insist upon instead was party orthodoxy, as they defined it. Ignoring the plain fact that for Douglas, opposition to the Lecompton constitution had been a matter, not only of principle, but also of political survival, they branded him a traitor. And ignoring the fact that the Freeport doctrine was actually of southern origin, they branded him a heretic. As punishment, the Senate Democratic leadership in December 1858 stripped him of his chairmanship of the committee on territories, a position that he had held continuously for more than ten years.[23]

Douglas responded with his usual vigor and combativeness. The southern Democrats, in turn, set out to make approval of a territorial slave code the supreme test of party loyalty. That was the ostensible issue that eventually disrupted the party at Charleston, but the real issue was Douglas, and the purpose of the slave-code agitation was to destroy him as a presidential candidate.

Of course, the South never approached unanimity in such matters, and the Little Giant continued to have supporters in every southern state right down to 1860. Even the Lower South gave him 11 percent of its total popular vote for president that year. One is nevertheless struck by the volume and intensity of southern hatred for Douglas in the period 1858–1860. He was with us, the indictment ran, "until the time of trial came; then he deceived and betrayed us." He "placed himself at the head of the Black column and gave the word of command," thereby becoming "stained with the dishonor of treachery without a parallel in the political history of the country." And now, covered with the "odium of . . . detestable heresies" and the "filth of his defiant recreancy," he would receive what southern patriots had always given northern enemies—"war to the knife." Then, "away with him to the tomb which he is digging for his political corpse."[24]

In retrospect, it appears that the only hope of preventing a Republican presidential victory lay in uniting the Democratic party behind Douglas. Yet, by 1860, southern hostility toward Douglas had taken on a life of its own and become implacable. The motives of southern leaders at this point are not easily fathomed or summarized. Perhaps as many as a score of them harbored serious presidential aspirations and so had personal reasons for wanting Douglas out of the way. There were also committed secessionists working openly to disrupt the Democratic party and welcoming the likelihood of a Republican presidential victory as the best means of achieving disunion. Covertly or subconsciously allied with them was a larger group of southerners (including Jefferson Davis, for example) who continued to call secession a "last resort," while conducting themselves in a way that tended to eliminate other choices. Their "conditional Unionism" with impossible conditions amounted to secessionism in the end.

But in addition to all the purposes visible in southern attitudes toward Douglas, his defection had an important symbolic meaning that weighed heavily on the southern spirit. The theme of betrayal and fear of betrayal runs prominently through much of the southern rhetoric of alienation. The South had been betrayed, in a sense, by its own ancestors who first accepted the role of slaveholder. It felt betrayed by New England, whose abolitionist zealots now made war on an institution introduced into the country by New England slave traders. It felt betrayed by Taylor as president and by Walker as territorial governor of Kansas. Southerners also feared treachery from their slaves and free blacks. They distrusted the sectional loyalty of nonslaveholding southern whites, and in the Lower South there was strong doubt that the border states could be depended upon in a crisis.

In such a context, the defection of Douglas was an especially painful blow. Perhaps no single event contributed so much to the southern sense of being isolated in a hostile world. "[It] has done more than all else," wrote a South Carolinian, "to shake my confidence in Northern men on the slavery issue, for I have long regarded him as one of our . . . most reliable friends." A correspondent of the Charleston *Mercury* put it more tersely: "If he proved false, whom can you trust?"[25] To despair of Douglas was virtually to despair of the Union itself. At the Charleston convention in the spring of 1860, the states of the Lower South withdrew from the Democratic party organization rather than submit to the nomination of Douglas. Who could then doubt that those same states would withdraw from the Union rather than submit to the election of a Republican president? In this respect, the dramatic walkout of delegates at Charleston was a dress rehearsal for secession.

The final crisis of the Union is commonly thought of as starting with the election of Lincoln in November 1860, but the entire presidential campaign had taken place in an atmosphere of crisis that extended back into the preceding year. When the Thirty-sixth Congress convened on December 5, 1859, John Brown was just three days in his grave, and the storm of emotion caused by his adventure at Harpers Ferry had not yet begun to abate. The House of Representatives plunged immediately into a two-month-long speakership contest of such bitterness that many members of Congress armed themselves for protection against assault. One senator, with grim hyperbole, said that the only persons not carrying a revolver and a knife were those carrying two revolvers.

Then, after an angry renewal of the slave-code debate in the Senate, there came the splitting of the Democratic party at Charleston. By midsummer, many southerners recognized that the odds strongly favored a Republican victory, and they began, in their minds, at least, to prepare for it. October elections for state offices in Pennsylvania and Indiana turned probability almost into certainty, and still there was another month left for preparation.

Meanwhile, with the apprehension aroused by John Brown still keenly felt, a new wave of fear swept through the South. There were reports of slaves in revolt, of conspiracies uncovered just in time, of mass poisonings attempted, of whole towns burned, and of abolitionist agents caught and hung. And the full terror, presumably, still lay ahead. "If such things come upon us," said a Georgia newspaper, "with only the *prospect* of an Abolition ruler, what will be our condition when he is *actually in power?*"[26] The very vagueness of the prospect made it all the more ominous. Fear of Republican rule was to no small degree a fear of the unknown. Chief Justice Roger B. Taney was not alone in believing that the news of Lincoln's election might be the signal for a general slave uprising. But other prophets of doom, like the editors of the Richmond *Enquirer*, pictured Republican purposes working out in more insidious ways:

> Upon the accession of Lincoln to power, we would apprehend no direct act of violence against negro property, but by the use of federal office, contracts, power and patronage, the building up in every Southern State of a Black Republican party, the ally and stipendiary of Northern fanaticism, to become in a few short years the open advocates of abolition. . . . No act of violence may ever be committed, no servile war waged, and yet the ruin and degradation of Virginia will be as fully and fatally accomplished, as though bloodshed and rapine ravished the land.[27]

One wonders how often in history rebellions and other cataclysmic events have not occurred, even in the presence of adequate causes, simply because there was no practical point of impulse where feeling and belief could be translated into action. For southerners, the presidential election of 1860 was just such a point of impulse—its date fixed on the calendar, its outcome predictable and not subject to compromise, its expected consequences vague but terrible. All the passion of the sectional conflict became concentrated, like the sun's rays by a magnifying glass, on one moment of decision that could come only once in history—that is, the *first* election of a Republican president. If secessionists had not seized the moment but instead had somehow been persuaded to let it pass, such a clear signal for action might never again have sounded.

Yet, even under these optimum conditions created by Lincoln's election, the southern will to act was but partly energized. The South, though long united in defense of slavery, had never been close to unity on the subject of secession. And so, in the end, the best fuse available set off only half of the accumulated charge. Just the seven states of the Lower South broke away from the Union in the winter of 1860–1861, although their very number, as I have already suggested, probably had a critical influence on the subsequent course of events.

But if only the Lower South seceded, the entire Slaveholding South had contributed heavily to the event that activated the secession movement—that is, to the Republican capture of the presidency. In 1852, the Free Soil candidate for president received only 7 percent of the popular vote in the free states and did not come close to winning a single electoral vote. Just eight years later, Lincoln won 55 percent of the popular vote in the free states and 98 percent of their electoral vote. It is difficult to believe that a political revolution of such magnitude would have occurred if southerners had not chosen to pursue the will-o'-the-wisp of Kansas, sacrificing the realities of power to an inner need for reassurance of their equal status and moral respectability in the face of antislavery censure.

The Charleston *Mercury*, commenting on the Dred Scott decision in 1857, said that it was "a victory more fatal, perhaps, than defeat," because the antislavery forces always rose up stronger after each sectional confrontation and, in fact, seemed to feed on adversity.[28] Pursuing the same theme more than a century later, David M. Potter wrote:

For ten years the Union had witnessed a constant succession of crises; always these ended in some kind of "victory" for the South, each of which left the South with an empty prize and left the Union in a weaker condition than before. . . . Not one of [the victories] added anything to the area, the strength, the influence, or even the security of the southern system. Yet each had cost the South a high price, both in alienating the public opinion of the nation and in weakening . . . the Democratic party, which alone stood between the South and sectional domination by the Republicans.[29]

Yet the victories of the South, though useless, were not meaningless. Important values seemed to be at stake—values associated, above all, with regional and personal self-respect. More than one southern political leader insisted that the fight for the Lecompton constitution had to be made because it was a "point of honor." With the same sensitivity about honor and the same disregard for possible consequences, many a southerner had faced his opponent on the dueling ground.

In the spring of 1861, with secession accomplished and the Confederate States of America a functioning reality, there remained still another point of honor to be settled, another empty prize to be won at exorbitant cost. It appears now that the Confederacy's best hope of survival may have been to avoid war and consolidate its independent status as long as possible, rather than trying to win a war against a stronger enemy. But the stars and stripes still flying on a fortified island in Charleston Harbor had become an infuriating symbol of southern independence unrecognized and thus another instance of southern honor degraded. So, in the early morning of April 12, 1861, southerners once again did what they had to do. They opened fire on Fort Sumter and this time gained a military victory more disastrous, perhaps, than any of their later military defeats.

Appendix

◆――――――

The following summary of southern roll call votes in Congress is based (with one correction) upon tables in Glover Moore, *The Missouri Controversy, 1819–1821* (Lexington: University of Kentucky Press, 1966), pages 53, 55, 109, 111, and Holman Hamilton, *Prologue to Conflict: The Crisis and Compromise of 1850* (Lexington: University of Kentucky Press, 1964), pages 191–92, 195–200. In each instance, the affirmative vote is given first. The eight measures included are:

1. The clause of the Tallmadge proviso that forbade the further introduction of slavery into Missouri. It passed the House on February 17, 1819, by a vote of 87 to 76, and was rejected in the Senate on February 27 by a vote of 22 to 16.
2. The clause of the Tallmadge proviso that freed slave children born after the date of admission when they had reached the age of twenty-five. It passed the House on February 17, 1819, by a vote of 82 to 78, and was rejected in the Senate on February 27 by a vote of 31 to 7.
3. The Thomas amendment prohibiting slavery "forever" in that part of the Louisiana Purchase lying north of 36° 30′ (Missouri excepted). It was approved in the Senate on Febru-

ary 17, 1820, by a vote of 14 to 8, and passed the House on March 2 by a vote of 134 to 42.

4. The admission of California to statehood, which passed the Senate on August 13, 1850, by a vote of 34 to 18, and passed the House on September 7 by a vote of 150 to 56.

5. The organization of Utah Territory without any slavery restriction. It passed the Senate on July 31, 1850, by a vote of 32 to 18, and passed the House on September 7 by a vote of 97 to 85.

6. The organization of New Mexico Territory without any slavery restriction. It passed the Senate on August 15, 1850, by a vote of 27 to 10, and passed the House (where it was linked with the Senate bill settling the problems of the Texas debt and boundary) on September 6 by a vote of 108 to 97.

7. Abolition of the slave trade in the District of Columbia, passed by the Senate on September 16, 1850, by a vote of 33 to 19, and passed by the House on September 17, by a vote of 124 to 59.

8. The Fugitive Slave Act, passed by the Senate on August 23, 1850, by a vote of 27 to 12, and passed by the House on September 12 by a vote of 109 to 76.

**Southern Congressional Voting on Slavery
in 1819–1820 and 1850**
(House and Senate Combined)

	Lower South	*Middle South*	*Border South*	*Totals*
Tallmadge–1	0–18	0–43	1–22	1–83
Tallmadge–2	0–18	0–43	2–20	2–81
36° 30′	12–14	17–29	22–2	51–45
California	1–39	11–29	21–6	33–74
Utah	23–12	31–4	23–1	77–17
New Mexico	15–19	29–10	24–1	68–30
D.C.	1–33	3–33	6–12	10–78
Fug. Slave	38–0	41–0	23–0	102–0

Notes

◈————

Introduction

1. David Donald, "American Historians and the Causes of the Civil War," *South Atlantic Quarterly*, LIX (1960), 351.

2. Avery O. Craven, *An Historian and the Civil War* (Chicago: University of Chicago Press, 1964), 1.

3. Joel H. Silbey, "The Civil War Synthesis in American Political History," *Civil War History*, X (1964), 140.

4. Eric Foner, "The Causes of the American Civil War: Recent Interpretations and New Directions," *Civil War History*, XX (1974), 197–98, 201–203.

5. Craven, *An Historian and the Civil War*, 232–33.

6. Foner, "Causes of the Civil War," 203.

7. Carl N. Degler, "The Two Cultures and the Civil War," in Stanley Coben and Lorman Ratner (eds.), *The Development of an American Culture* (Englewood Cliffs, N.J.: Prentice Hall, 1970), 92.

8. David Brion Davis, *The Problem of Slavery in Western Culture* (Ithaca, N.Y.: Cornell University Press, 1966); and *The Problem of Slavery in the Age of Revolution, 1770–1823* (Ithaca, N.Y.: Cornell University Press, 1975).

9. William L. Barney, *The Secessionist Impulse: Alabama and Mississippi in 1860* (Princeton: Princeton University Press, 1974), 313.

10. South Carolina, because of its experience with nullification, its premier leadership in secession, and its central role in the Fort Sumter crisis, might very well be treated as a category all by itself. In South Carolina, slaves were 57 percent of the population in 1860.

11. Avery O. Craven, *The Growth of Southern Nationalism, 1848–1861* (Baton Rouge: Louisiana State University Press, 1953), x.

12. The Georgia platform, a series of resolutions adopted by a convention called to consider the Compromise of 1850, named the following potential actions of Congress as sufficient in each case to justify secession: (1) abolition of slavery in the District of Columbia without the consent of its inhabitants; (2) abolition on federally owned property in the South; (3) suppression of the domestic slave trade; (4) refusal to admit a new slave state; (5) prohibition of slavery in the territories of New Mexico and Utah; (6) repeal or significant modification of the fugitive-slave laws.

Chapter 1

1. James A. Woodburn, "The Historical Significance of the Missouri Compromise," in *Annual Report of the American Historical Association for 1893* (Washington, D.C.: American Historical Association, 1894), 294.

2. Clement Eaton, *A History of the Old South* (2nd ed.; New York: Macmillan, 1966), 4.

3. Charles S. Sydnor, *The Development of Southern Sectionalism, 1819–1848* (Baton Rouge: Louisiana State University Press, 1948), 32.

4. Jesse T. Carpenter, *The South as a Conscious Minority, 1789–1861* (New York: New York University Press, 1930), 4.

5. John Richard Alden, *The First South* (Baton Rouge: Louisiana State University Press, 1961), 4.

6. Jefferson to John Taylor, June 1, 1798, in Paul Leicester Ford (ed.), *The Writings of Thomas Jefferson* (10 vols; New York: G. P. Putnam's Sons, 1892–99), VII, 263.

7. Jefferson to Stephens Thompson Mason, October 11, 1798, in *ibid.*, VII, 283.

8. *Annals of Congress*, 8th Cong., 2nd Sess., 1567–70.

9. For the rationalization of his silence on slavery during the presidential years, see Jefferson to George Logan, May 11, 1805, Ford (ed.), *Writings of Jefferson*, VIII, 351–52. On the subject generally, see John Chester Miller, *The Wolf by the Ears: Thomas Jefferson and Slavery* (New York: Free Press, 1977).

10. *Annals of Congress*, 8th Cong., 1st Sess., 241–42; Don E. Fehrenbacher, *The Dred Scott Case: Its Significance in American Law and Politics* (New York: Oxford University Press, 1978), 91–100.

11. *Annals of Congress*, 15th Cong., 1st Sess., 1675–76.

12. In New York especially, Republican factionalism strengthened the influence of dying Federalism. The followers of Governor DeWitt Clinton, widely regarded as Federalists at heart, lent strong support to the antislavery movement. See Shaw Livermore, Jr., *The Twilight of Federalism: The Disin-*

tegration of the Federalist Party, 1815–1830 (Princeton: Princeton University Press, 1962), 69–74; Glover Moore, *The Missouri Controversy, 1819–1821* (Lexington: University of Kentucky Press, 1966), 16–17.

13. Thomas D. Morris, *Free Men All: The Personal Liberty Laws of the North, 1780–1861* (Baltimore: Johns Hopkins University Press, 1974), 35–41; *Annals of Congress*, 15th Cong., 2nd Sess., 306, 311.

14. Southerners voted sixty-six to one against the first clause of the Tallmadge proviso and sixty-four to two against the second. Moore, *Missouri Controversy*, 53*n*.

15. *Annals of Congress*, 16th Cong., 1st Sess., 427, for the text of the 36° 30' restriction, which is often called the Thomas Amendment because it was introduced by Jesse B. Thomas, Virginia-born senator from Illinois.

16. Moore, *Missouri Controversy*, 129–69.

17. *Annals of Congress*, 16th Cong., 1st Sess., 1391.

18. *Ibid.*, 16th Cong., 1st Sess., 468, 1586–87.

19. *Ibid.*, 16th Cong., 1st Sess., 428, 1587–88.

20. Moore, *Missouri Controversy*, 108.

21. Imprecise because it seems likely that some southern members of the House who voted against the 36° 30' restriction by itself would have voted in favor of the Compromise package if they had had the opportunity. This, at least, was the case in the Senate, where southerners voted only fourteen to eight in favor of the 36° 30' restriction, but twenty to two in favor of the Compromise as a whole. *Annals of Congress*, 16th Cong., 1st Sess., 428.

22. Moore, *Missouri Controversy*, 242.

23. Richmond *Enquirer*, February 10, 1820.

24. Moore, *Missouri Controversy*, 177.

25. *Annals of Congress*, 16th Cong., 1st Sess., 1578, 1582.

26. *Ibid.*, 16th Cong., 1st Sess., 175; *ibid.*, 15th Cong., 2nd Sess., 1204.

27. Richmond *Enquirer*, March 7, 1820.

28. Moore, *Missouri Controversy*, 175.

29. *Congressional Globe*, 35th Cong., 1st Sess., 773.

30. Moore, *Missouri Controversy*, 348.

31. *Annals of Congress*, 16th Cong., 1st Sess., 1025.

Chapter 2

1. *Congressional Globe*, 31st Cong., 1st Sess., 28, 1216.

2. *Ibid.*, 31st Cong., 1st Sess., 259; Joseph Carlyle Sitterson, *The Secession Movement in North Carolina* (Chapel Hill: University of North Carolina Press, 1939), 69–70; Ulrich B. Phillips (ed.), *The Correspondence of Robert Toombs, Alexander H. Stephens, and Howell Cobb*, in *Annual Report of the American Historical Association for 1911* (2 vols.; Washington, D.C.: Ameri-

can Historical Association, 1912), II, 183; Jefferson Davis, *The Rise and Fall of the Confederate Government* (2 vols.; New York: D. Appleton, 1881), I, 83.

3. *Congressional Globe*, 29th Cong., 2nd Sess., 454.

4. Missouri was admitted August 10, 1821; the Wilmot Proviso was introduced August 8, 1846.

5. Beveridge to Beard, March 16, 1926, Albert J. Beveridge Papers, Manuscript Division, Library of Congress.

6. Chauncey C. Boucher and Robert P. Brooks (eds.), *Correspondence Addressed to John C. Calhoun, 1837–1849*, in *Annual Report of the American Historical Association for 1929* (2 vols.; Washington, D.C.: American Historical Association, 1930), II, 385–87.

7. *Congressional Globe*, 31st Cong., 1st Sess., 235.

8. *Ibid.*, 36th Cong., 2nd Sess., 56.

9. *Ibid.*, 31st Cong., 1st Sess., 236.

10. Henry Steele Commager (ed.), *Documents of American History* (7th ed.; 2 vols.; New York: Appleton-Century-Crofts, 1963), I, 373–74.

11. Richmond *Enquirer*, February 19, 1847.

12. *Congressional Globe*, 31st Cong., 1st Sess., 29. See also William J. Cooper, Jr., *The South and the Politics of Slavery, 1828–1856* (Baton Rouge: Louisiana State University Press, 1978), 240.

13. Arthur Bestor, "State Sovereignty and Slavery: A Reinterpretation of Proslavery Constitutional Doctrine, 1846–1860," *Journal of the Illinois State Historical Society*, LIV (1961), 147.

14. *Congressional Globe*, 29th Cong., 2nd Sess., 455, for Calhoun's resolutions of February 19, 1847.

15. *Ibid.*, 29th Cong., 2nd Sess., 187; *ibid.*, 30th Cong., 1st Sess., 1062–63; Don E. Fehrenbacher, *The Dred Scott Case: Its Significance in American Law and Politics* (New York: Oxford University Press, 1978), 132–33, 147–51.

16. David M. Potter, *The Impending Crisis, 1848–1861*, completed and edited by Don E. Fehrenbacher (New York: Harper and Row, 1976), 73–75; Robert W. Johannsen, *Stephen A. Douglas* (New York: Oxford University Press, 1973), 242.

17. *Congressional Globe*, 31st Cong., 1st Sess., 203.

18. Richard Malcolm Johnston and William Hand Browne (eds.), *Life of Alexander H. Stephens* (rev. ed.; Philadelphia: J. B. Lippincott, 1883), 238–39.

19. Holman Hamilton, *Prologue to Conflict: The Crisis and Compromise of 1850* (Lexington: University of Kentucky Press, 1964), 54.

20. Fehrenbacher, *Dred Scott Case*, 162–63. Tables of voting are in Hamilton, *Prologue to Conflict*, 191–200.

21. Phillips (ed.), *Correspondence of Toombs, Stephens, and Cobb*, 283.

22. Robert R. Russel, "What Was the Compromise of 1850?" *Journal of*

Southern History, XXII (1956), 292–309. For a critique, see Fehrenbacher, *Dred Scott Case*, 174–76.

23. *Harper's New Monthly Magazine*, IV (1851), 120, calculated that recent elections in the four states had resulted in 110,882 secessionist votes out of a total of 261,388 (about 42 percent). But see Cooper, *South and the Politics of Slavery*, 309, where it is maintained that the elections were not a confrontation between Unionists and disunionists.

24. Phillips (ed.), *Correspondence of Toombs, Stephens, and Cobb*, 249–59.

25. Potter, *Impending Crisis*, 143–44.

26. Richard Harrison Shryock, *Georgia and the Union in 1850* (Durham, N.C.: Duke University Press, 1926), 344.

Chapter 3

1. *Congressional Globe*, 27th Cong., 3rd Sess., App., 103.

2. Jesse T. Carpenter, *The South as a Conscious Minority, 1789–1861* (New York: New York University Press, 1930), 180–81.

3. David M. Potter, *The Impending Crisis, 1848–1861*, completed and edited by Don E. Fehrenbacher (New York: Harper and Row, 1976), 235–38, but cf. Michael F. Holt, *The Political Crisis of the 1850's* (New York: John Wiley and Sons, 1978), 102, 118–19. Holt advances a striking new thesis that the second American party system collapsed in the 1850s "because Whig and Democratic voters lost faith in their old parties as adequate vehicles for effective political action."

4. See Potter, *Impending Crisis*, 238–47; Holt, *Political Crisis*, 154–69.

5. John V. Mering, "The Slave-State Constitutional Unionists and the Politics of Consensus," *Journal of Southern History*, XLIII (1977), 398. See also William J. Cooper, Jr., *The South and the Politics of Slavery, 1828–1856* (Baton Rouge: Louisiana State University Press, 1978), 372–73.

6. *Congressional Globe*, 33rd Cong., 1st Sess., 1254; Potter, *Impending Crisis*, 167n.

7. William L. Barney, *The Road to Secession: A New Perspective on the Old South* (New York: Praeger Publishers, 1972), 6, and William L. Barney, *The Secessionist Impulse: Alabama and Mississippi in 1860* (Princeton: Princeton University Press, 1974), 16.

8. Don E. Fehrenbacher, "Disunion and Reunion," in John Higham (ed.), *The Reconstruction of American History* (New York: Harper and Row, 1962), 102.

9. Avery O. Craven, *The Growth of Southern Nationalism, 1848–1861* (Baton Rouge: Louisiana State University Press, 1953), 196. But cf. Cooper, *The South and the Politics of Slavery*, 352n, where Craven's interpretation is disputed.

10. Craven, *Growth of Southern Nationalism*, 394.
11. George Harmon Knoles (ed.), *The Crisis of the Union, 1860–1861* (Baton Rouge: Louisiana State University Press, 1965), 88.
12. The support of the Lower South was in fact unanimous. Of the 145 anti-Lecompton votes in both houses, 10 were cast by southerners—8 from the Border South and 2 from the Middle South. *Congressional Globe*, 35th Cong., 1st Sess., 1264–65, 1437.
13. *Ibid.*, 35th Cong., 1st Sess., 393.
14. *Ibid.*, 35th Cong., 1st Sess., 858.
15. James D. Tradewell to Hammond, February 11, 1858, James H. Hammond Papers, Manuscript Division, Library of Congress.
16. James D. Richardson (ed.), *A Compilation of the Messages and Papers of the Presidents* (11 vols.; Washington: Government Printing Office, 1913), IV, 3011.
17. W. D. Porter to James H. Hammond, January 30, 1858, Hammond Papers.
18. Ulrich B. Phillips (ed.), *The Correspondence of Robert Toombs, Alexander H. Stephens, and Howell Cobb*, in *Annual Report of the American Historical Association for 1911* (2 vols.; Washington, D.C.: American Historical Association, 1912), II, 432, 434.
19. Richardson (ed.), *Messages and Papers of the Presidents*, IV, 2963.
20. See above, p. 7.
21. Joseph Carlyle Sitterson, *The Secession Movement in North Carolina* (Chapel Hill: University of North Carolina Press, 1939), 135.
22. John Bassett Moore (ed.), *The Works of James Buchanan* (12 vols.; Philadelphia: Lippincott, 1908–11), X, 229.
23. Robert W. Johannsen, *Stephen A. Douglas* (New York: Oxford University Press, 1973), 685–87.
24. Don E. Fehrenbacher, *The Dred Scott Case: Its Influence in American Law and Politics* (New York: Oxford University Press, 1978), 468, 483–84.
25. W. D. Porter to James H. Hammond, December 28, 1857, Hammond Papers; Charleston *Mercury*, January 16, 1858. For other similar comments, see Harold S. Schultz, *Nationalism and Sectionalism in South Carolina, 1852–1860* (Durham, N.C.: Duke University Press, 1950), 168–69.
26. Ollinger Crenshaw, *The Slave States in the Presidential Election of 1860* (Baltimore: Johns Hopkins Press, 1945), 104*n*.
27. July 10, 1860, in Dwight Lowell Dumond (ed.), *Southern Editorials on Secession* (New York: Century, 1931), 141.
28. Charleston *Mercury*, April 20, 21, 1857.
29. Potter, *Impending Crisis*, 325–26.

Index

◆————

DATE DUE

| | |